CHAKRA

RADIATE POSITIVE ENERGY WITH YOGA MEDITATION

Huor Calaelen

CONTENT

INTRODUCTION

The word chakra in Sanskrit means "spinning wheel". The technique consists in turning these wheels one after the other. Thus the chakras harmonize one after the other to allow the vital energy to flow and the different bodies to be aligned. After a while, you will feel this energy circulating.

We speak of seven main chakras and thousands of secondary chakras. Each chakra is associated with an organ of action, a sensory organ, a color, a sound, an element. They are aligned like a light column starting from the bottom up. We will only talk about the seven main ones, the most important ones.

Before meditation there are two things to do. Take three good breaths to relax and anchor. We imagine roots coming out of our feet and descending deeply into the earth until we reach the Earth's core. You imagine surrounding this one. During the inspiration you visualize a red color going up in these roots, which represents the sap, you will be fed good telluric energies.

It goes back to the first chakra (in the basin). And exhale everything you do not need. Then we will do the same thing with the other chakras, with their respective colors starting from the bottom up. So orange, yellow, green, light blue, dark blue and mauve

CHAPTER ONE

ABOUT THE CHAKRAS

From the etymological point of view, it is the Sanskrit name given to circular objects. As an integral part of Hindu (and Buddhist) belief, chakras have been a foundation of traditional Ayurvedic medicine for over five millennia. They designate the junction points of energy channels, an energetic vortex belonging to the "subtle body" of the human being invisible to the naked eye.

These junction points are also used in traditional Chinese medicine, especially in the practice of acupuncture. According to some beliefs, the chakras represent the energy of the etheric life force as well as part of the soul. Their main function is to promote the circulation of vital energy (also called prana or chi) between different physical organs. Aligned on the spine, they function in a complementary and interdependent way, and form a bridge between the spiritual and the physical.

MEANING CHAKRA

Chakra is called a wheel. Like a wheel that turns and can whirl things away, like a car that stirs up dust. Like the wheel, Chakra emits prana, meaning life energy. The chakras are also referred to as patmas, that is, as lotuses. Just as a lotus can open, unfold and look beautiful, but can also be closed as a bud, so chakras can be closed and have a lot of greatness in them. When we practice yoga, then the lotus opens, the chakra opens and much greatness can come into being.

There are many chakras. In the last lecture, I talked about the nadis that transport prana, the life energy. The life energy is stored in the energy points of the nadis. The energy points of the nadis are called chakras. Chakras are actually a collective name for many energy points. Every point where the Prana gathers is a chakra.

The Marmas in Ayurveda are so chakras. Or the acupuncture points are all chakras. Whenever two nadis cross, a chakra is created again. This chakra then determines how the prana is distributed between the nadis and how the prana passes from one nadi to another.

Since there are 72,000 nadis and different chakras in each nadi, there are many chakras. The chakras may be transitional centers, from which the prana passes from one nadi to another.

They can also be sources of power - pranic springs - through which Prana is absorbed. And there are tongue chakras where energy is absorbed through food, through liquids. The hand chakras can both absorb energy as well as radiate it. Then there are the chakras, which are energy stores, much like accumulators.

Chakras are also the organs of the astral body; one could say that all emotional centers are chakras, and all mental faculties are also developed thanks to the chakras. Then there are hidden abilities that can still be developed when the chakras open completely.

So there are a lot of effects of chakras and they are also the connections from the astral body to the physical body. Some chakras can also control or influence physical organs. Other chakras are responsible for emotions and for mental abilities. And again other chakras are simply accumulators or compounds in the fines , in the Pranamayakosha.

The Earth's magnetic field is a good example of energy flow. The energy flow enters from the bottom, traverses the disk vertically, appears from the side up and down, and from the bottom up. In the human body, this is exactly the energy flow of each chakra.

The term is better known today as "spiritual centers" or "points of junction of energy channels (nāḍī)" derived from a conception of Kundalini yoga and which could be localized in the human body. According to this conception, there would be seven main chakras and thousands of secondary chakras.

It is a symbol of power Chakra (wheel) in the center of the flag of India.

In ancient India, the word meant a metal disk - gold, copper or iron - symbolizing the power of a Raja said chakravarti: one who turns the wheel of the destiny of men, holding their lives in his hands, but also, perhaps, one who is in the image of sūrya, the sun. The title of chakravarti or chakravartin was given to a sovereign who had sacrificed the horse or made great conquests.

The disc is the main attribute of the god Vishnu.

In Hinduism, the wheel represents the structure of the worlds and the individual, "whose core is the heart, the rays its faculties and the points of contact with the rim the organs of perception and action.

The term was then used to describe Buddha and the Buddhist rulers, who turn the wheel of the law (dharma chakra-mudra gesture).

We thus find very logically a representation of chakra in the emblem and the flag of India. In the beginning, Gandhi's spinning wheel, the emblematic tool of self-sufficiency, was to be found in the white band. It was later replaced by the chakra of Ashoka, a Buddhist symbol, under the influence of B. R. Ambedkar, editor outcaste of the Indian Constitution which eventually converts to Buddhism.

THE PROPERTIES OF EACH CHAKRA

All chakras have unique properties and specific functions, and the activity level of these depends on their health. The chakras also have a link with the frequency of the vibrations and they are in charge of supplying different parts of the body with energy. When a chakra is open or active and the energy flows freely, this indicates its health. If the chakra is closed, clogged, stagnant or dark, or even over-stimulated, it indicates that there is a problem somewhere.

The chakras are directly related to our physical, mental, emotional body as well as all the subtle bodies. It would surely be difficult to list all the properties of these because there is a large amount and research continues to discover new ones. Here are the main properties and keywords that will help you start your chakra discovery.

SEVENTH: CROWN CHAKRA

The crown chakra is a link with the invisible world. When the chakra is open, we receive information from the invisible world through the chakra channel and let in the light of the universe. This light is pure Love.

On the contrary, when our chakra is closed or plugged, it is usually due to the conditioning of society that prevents it from believing anything other than science or physical and tangible evidence. People are almost always born closed, disconnected. Thus, when our crown is closed, it is more difficult to believe and especially to feel our unity with life. We feel divided and we are filled with fears and illusions that condition to the society of "subway, work, sleep" and an education too rigid and far from the truth.

SIXTH: CHAKRA OF THE THIRD EYE

The third eye chakra is connected to the eyes, nose and nervous system. It stimulates both hemispheres of the brain. All organs connected to the third eye are affected by it. When the third eye chakra is unbalanced, there may be a problem with the eyes, sinuses, head (fog or mental fatigue), difficulty in being positive and learning and concentration disorder.

The sixth chakra stimulates our inner senses, enabling us to attain greater awareness and greater access to the unseen and the truth. Although it is not the only chakra responsible for our intuition, it plays a big role. The third eye activates the extra-perception and it says that it also activates all the other chakras. When our third eye is open and healthy, we have more intuition, imagination, creativity, clarity and energy.

FIFTH: CHAKRA OF THE THROAT

By stimulating the throat chakra, we facilitate verbal communication, breathing, throat and neck health and the ability to swallow. By swallowing, it does not only mean swallowing food or liquid, but also swallowing the situations and information we receive on a daily basis, and then digesting them (accepting them).

If an event such as the death of a loved one is too difficult to swallow for an individual, it will be difficult to let the information in and therefore the throat will have difficulty passing the information. If the person has difficulty expressing himself, his throat may be in pain. These are just a few examples of the many functions of the throat.

FOURTH: HEART CHAKRA

The heart chakra, as the name says, is connected to the heart. A healthy heart chakra is a heart filled with peace, love, compassion and generosity. The person feels in harmony with life, with situations that arise and emotions based on love. Love for others always starts with self-love.

A closed or stagnant heart chakra is a sign of inner torment, jealousy, anxiety and sadness that can result in isolation.

THIRD: SOLAR PLEXUS CHAKRA

The third chakra is the solar plexus, centrally located just below the ribcage. This chakra is further affected by what we eat as food and the quantity of it. It is also known that the plexus is the most favorable place for rejected and repressed emotions. Thus, a person is afraid of experiencing sadness, he represses his solar plexus.

When we open the solar plexus chakra, it is almost inevitable that the emotions will come out too. They go out to heal. The energy that flows in a chakra when opened, illuminates what is not light. The knots of emotions or toxins become clean light. Finally, the solar chakra is a very good teacher of acceptance and letting go.

SECOND: SACRED CHAKRA

The sacred chakra is directly related to vital energy, taste, desire, pleasure, creativity, and sexual organs. Observing one's desires is a way to see if the chakra is healthy.

Healthy desires are: to eat healthy, to have good sexual health, to take care of ourselves, etc. They relate to love, sensitivity and appreciation.

Unhealthy desires can be stimulated by an overactive chakra that causes excessiveness or not-enough-active chakra that causes depression. Unhealthy desires are: drugs or smoking, sexual dysfunction or insignificant sex, investing in gambling and even eating too much. These bring possessiveness, difficulty to disillusion, dissatisfaction and lack among other many consequences. These troubles quickly move us to the truth.

FIRST: ROOT CHAKRA

The root chakra is the bridge that binds us to the physical and material world. The energy of the root chakra is directly connected to the center of the Earth. The light of this chakra is red and it roots us. It is essential to be rooted to live healthy as human on Earth. On the contrary, being too rooted detaches us from the invisible world which is just as important as the visible. We must find the balance of the two.

Moreover, this chakra relates to the basic needs of the human. Like the sacred chakra, when it is too stimulated, there can be excess. This excess can be at the level of food, alcohol, money, sex and consumption. The feeling of security, the taste of the present moment and the unity with the Earth are the natural effects of an open and healthy root chakra.

HOW TO CLEAN CHAKRAS QUICKLY?

It is worth noticing that the 7 main chakras must be perfectly balanced to ensure good physical, spiritual, mental and emotional health. In case of a health problem - physical aches or pains, stress or spiritual blockage - the cleansing and healing of the main chakras are the best ways to break free. The best medicine is meditation.

1. THE ROOT CHAKRA OR MULADHARA

Located at the bottom of the spine, below the perineum, this is the basic support for the entire chakra system. At the root of every human being's survival instinct, the root chakra provides physical, emotional and mental well-being. Blockage or deficiency in this chakra can cause pain in the lumbar or bones, varicose veins in the legs, hemorrhoids, etc. From a psychological point of view, there is a lack of self-confidence and / or fighting spirit, depression, carelessness, etc.

To rebalance the root chakra, meditation is required to realize its immense potential and to build self-confidence. Physical activities are also essential, but without going into excess, as well as healthy hobbies such as gardening.

2. THE SACRED CHAKRA OR SVADHISHTHANA

Located under the navel, the sacred chakra is governed by the element Water. It represents the center of sexual and emotional energy. A surplus of energy can lead to hyper-emotionality and an obsession with sexuality. Inadequate energy causes impotence or decreased libido, withdrawal, depression, lack of openness and taste for life. Among the evils caused by an imbalance of Svadhishthana, we distinguish the gynecological and urinary disorders, as well as the problems of rheumatism, digestion, colon, etc.

Practicing meditation helps rebalance the sacred chakra. The operation consists of focusing on its location, the part below the navel, and imagining an orange orb around it, the color of Svadhishthana. Throughout the session, it is important to focus on your breathing by inhaling and exhaling deeply. Among the essential oils to be preferred are Ylang-Ylang, Jasmine, Rose, Patchouli, Sandalwood and Sage.

3. THE SOLAR PLEXUS CHAKRA OR MANIPURA

Located under the tip of the sternum, the solar plexus chakra is the center of emotions and energies. Used to activate the healing of all types of ills, it is at the origin of the personality of everyone. A surplus of energy causes aggression, the search for domination, as well as the tendency to denigrate oneself or to denigrate others. A lack of energy leads to loss of motivation and ambition, indecision, etc. Among the problems associated with blocking energy in Manipura, there are bulimia, anorexia, arthritis, intestinal disorders or respiratory problems, among others.

During the meditation session, simply sit comfortably and visualize a golden orb in the center of the solar plexus chakra, intended to warm the body. Here are the essential oils to favor: cedar wood, cypress, elemi, ginger, mint, grapefruit and Ylang-Ylang.

4. THE HEART CHAKRA OR ANAHATA

As its name suggests, it is located at the heart level. It acts as a bridge between the six other chakras, including 3 below and 3 above. Essential to personal fulfillment, it is at the origin of feelings of love and compassion. If a surplus of energy causes an excess of these feelings, the lack causes jealousy, hatred and paranoia. Heart disease and back pain are some of the physical ailments associated with the heart chakra.

To rebalance the energy, it is recommended to practice meditation focusing on the heart center while imagining a golden orb that envelops the entire body. Essential oils recommended for the session include rosewood, cypress, lavender, patchouli and ylang-ylang.

5. THE THROAT CHAKRA OR VISHUDDHA

Considered the chakra of communication and creativity, it is located at the beginning of the gorge. It allows externalizing thoughts, knowledge and emotions, both by speech and gestures. A surplus of energy leads to arrogance, lack of listening and mythomania, while a blockage is causing difficulties in expressing oneself and lack of assurance. An imbalance can cause neck pain. , migraine and dysfunction of the thyroid gland

During meditation, focus on the starting part of the heart, crossing the throat and ending at the center of the head. It is important to breathe deeply and to imagine a blue light circulating all along these three zones. From the body. Here are the essential oils to use: lemon, cypress, incense, geranium, mint (peppery or green) and sage.

6. THE THIRD EYE CHAKRA OR AJNA

Located between the eyebrows, the third eye chakra represents self-awareness, sensory perception and creativity. Considered as the sixth sense, it allows one to develop one's healing power over oneself and others (at a distance). A surplus of energy leads to narcissism and the intellectual superiority complex, while a deficiency causes blindness, dyslexia and learning difficulties, as well as lack of intuition, personality and extra-sensory abilities.

Meditation should focus on reconnecting with one's body while focusing on the signs outside the physical body. It is important to trust your intuition and listen to the voice of your soul. Here are the essential oils to use: lemon, sandalwood, incense, juniper, bay leaf, patchouli, rosemary and clary sage.

7. THE CROWN CHAKRA OR SAHASRARA

Located at the top of the skull, it is the energy of enlightenment that connects every human being to the universe. It gives access to the subconscious and the unconscious to become aware of the beauty of everything around us. If the excess energy causes headaches and frustration, the deficiency results in the lack or lack of awareness of spirituality. The imbalance of Sahasrara is at the origin of suicidal ideation and loss of memory.

Meditation allows you to connect with the mind. During the session, it is necessary to visualize a light enveloping the top of the skull, destined to charge the physical and spiritual bodies. Among the essential oils to be favored are lime, cedar wood, sandalwood, helichrysum, gurjum, lavender and rose.

OTHER PRACTICES TO CLEAN THE CHAKRAS

In general, some activities can clean and rebalance the 7 chakras, including:

- Reiki
- The qi gong
- Yoga
- Lithotherapy
- Magnetism
- Sophrology
- Adopting a healthy diet and practicing physical activity is also a good way to maintain them.
- Clean up your chakras and rebalance your energy with the help of an online magnetizer

You feel a big drop in energy, you're off-center. Or you feel like you have no more control over your life: these are the signs that you need energy cleaning and rebalancing.

THE ORDER OF THE CHAKRAS

As you can see, the main chakras are numbered according to their position (1 to 7). When we meditate, it is better to start with the 7th chakra which is that of the crown, and to go down to the sixth, and so on. Of all the possible reasons for this order, there are two that are very simple.

First, we want energy to flow from head to toe. The light enters the head and flows into the feet. In this way, we end up rooted and somewhere else than in our head.

Secondly, to go into a deep trance in meditation makes it easier to slide down. This brings you to the depths of calm.

CHAKRAS, HOW DOES IT WORK

Transmitted by traditional Indian medicine more than 5,000 years ago, there are 88,000 chakras on the entire human body. But there are essentially seven main chakras, located from bottom to top of the spine. The energy passes from one chakra to another and creates an energetic field around the person. They feed and are powered by the energy of the body as a whole, on the principle of communicating vessels. A chakra testifies to our vitality and our openness to the experience of life.

INFLUENCE OF THE HEART CHAKRA ON ANTISOCIAL BEHAVIOR

The chakra of the heart is the fourth chakra, located in the center of the system of the 7 chakras. It acts on compassion, love and our relationships with others.

A blocked heart chakra can lead to antisocial behavior that can destroy a person away from their relationships.

The literal translation

For the traditional Sanskrit heart chakra is Anahata, which means "not struck".

It is easy to deduce that by balancing the chakra of the heart, one feels freer and opens up to others. In a sense, you will become "untouched" in your social life. Antisocial people are classified as not wanting to interact with others, but it's not limited to that. Maybe you feel like you cannot interact with others, you cannot create relationships, you do not feel that people really understand who you are, and you come to the conclusion that it's almost useless to create lasting links.

You may even feel so worried about people and relationships that it ends up being a heavy burden. If this describes how you feel lately, it could be the result of a deeper, more spiritual problem.

Symptoms of a blocked heart chakra may include:

- Co-addiction or rely on the approval of others
- Garder grudge and not be able to forgive
- Develop a victim mentality
- Response problems
- Cardiac diseases -Lack of empathy
- Being too critical

It is important to notice that these symptoms do not always occur when your heart chakra is blocked, and you may experience other symptoms apart from those mentioned above.

It is also important to put in evidence that there are two obvious extremes: either you feel complete isolation from others, or you will become so dependent on others you will lose yourself while seeking their approval.

The most important features of the heart chakra include:

- Mourning
- Compassion or empathy
- Compassionate discrimination
- Harmony and peace
- Ability to be loved and to love others
- Ability to forgive and accept others
- Creation of connections and of relationships
- Awareness and new perspectives

Essentially, the heart chakra is our path to creating lasting, emotional and deep bonds with the people around us. It fuses the functions of all the other chakras together, so it's the one that needs the most attention.

When the heart chakra is balanced, it also balances all the others, which means a healthy and happy life. When the heart chakra is blocked, you must be able to identify the problem in order to rebalance your world.

Try to eliminate as many sources of stress as possible in your life, in order to cleanse your heart chakra while trying to heal emotional pain.

Clinging to the emotional pain of the past is one of the most common ways to block your heart chakra and stumble on a dangerous path. Learn how to let go to open you.

THE STATE OF THE CHAKRAS

To easily understand what condition the chakras must be in order to work properly, the easiest way is to compare them to the tires of your car.

To work perfectly, a tire must receive a specific amount of air. It must be properly inflated.

Tires not enough or too inflated: problems of loss of grip, less effective braking, decreased longevity, increased fuel consumption, risk of tire burst and especially premature wear of the tire

A well-inflated tire wears evenly and lasts longer.

It is the same with the chakras; the difference is that we do not use the word "inflate" but "balance" what ultimately amounts to the same thing.

If a chakra is too "inflated" or under "inflated" there are problems of adhesion to life whereas if it is properly "inflated" it adheres perfectly.

Each chakra has a special function, so that the body works well, all the chakras must be balanced because they work together, the imbalance of one entails that of the others exactly like a car whose adhesion depends on the good use of all the tires.

Among the main functions of the chakras we find:

1st chakra, root chakra: security

2nd chakra, sacred chakra: vitality

3rd chakra, solar plexus chakra: personality

4th chakra, heart chakra: love

5th chakra, chakra of the throat: communication

6th chakra, 3rd eye chakra:

7th chakra thought, coronal chakra: acquaintance

When one of these chakras is unbalanced, what it represents will be deformed in excess or decrease. Thus a sub-activity of the 1st chakra will cause feelings of fear while an over-activity will cause an excess of self-confidence. Which in both cases creates a situation of poor adaptation to life, to keep a body in good health, in shape, in agreement with the world, it is necessary that all these chakras work in a balanced way and if they want to take you away, you have to take care exactly as you would with the tires of your car!

ROLE OF PRIMARY CHAKRAS AND SECONDARY CHAKRAS

Chakras are described as wheels of energy located at various points of the body. We also speak of chakras in the form of flowers with a number of petals according to the chakra, which is why we also speak of "opening" or "closing" a chakra, as a flower does.

There are seven major chakras and many secondary chakras, minor chakras, so the shoulder chakras , elbows, wrists, fingers are connected to the heart chakra , those of the hips, knees, ankles, toes and feet are connected at the 1st chakra, the root chakra , chakra of the base.

For the body to be stable there must be a good balance between the lower chakras and the upper chakras, in between the chakras located under the chakra of the heart and those located above.

Each chakra plays an emotional and relational role, depending on whether the energy circulates well or not and each of them is in synergy with an endocrine gland.

The endocrine glands discharge hormones into the blood and have an impact on the emotion and the psychological state of the individual.

The proper functioning of the chakras produces a feeling of well-being and the feeling of being in its place in the universe. Conversely, a psychological imbalance deteriorates the chakras.

It is important to balance the chakras because they act as communicating vessels, the energy circulates between them through communication channels called nadis, if a chakra lacks energy it will draw it in another chakra creating an imbalance because the functioning of some acts on that of others.

PRACTICAL EXERCISE

Here's a simple and effective practice that you can do in minutes.

- In meditation, visualize and feel one chakra at a time, starting with the crown chakra. You can visualize it as an open pipe that emits its own color: purple in the box of the crown chakra.
- The outline of the pipe has petals. Imagine these petals turning like propellers. They will help open and clean the chakra. The number of petals does not matter, because when they turn we do not count them.

- Let the images and the sensations of the circulating energy come and go, the cleaning and the fluidity of the propellers.
- Breathe inside the chakra.
- Step for the crown chakra only: Feel the white light of the universe flowing in the crown chakra that comes to awaken and stimulate all the other chakras.
- Repeat the same steps (without repeating step 5) with the sixth chakra, then the fifth, and so on.

CHAPTER TWO

ABOUT YOGA

Yoga is a practice of well-being and relaxation based on the liberation of chakras to resolve psychophysical tensions. We reveal the beneficial effects of yoga on both physical and mental fitness. Benefits, dangers, rates, different types of yoga

THE ORIGINS OF YOGA

Yoga is increasingly practiced more often for its physical benefits than for its benefits on the mind, yet both are related and the physical and mental state are improved at the same time after a few months of regular practice.

Some famous doctors see in Yoga a precious help to the prevention against certain chronic diseases. Yoga is a discipline aimed, through meditation, asceticism moral and physical exercises, to achieve the unification of the human being in its physical, mental and spiritual.

Yoga does not exclude the metaphysical plane of the physical plane and the mental plane. He does not separate matter from thought.

His method encompasses all knowledge, the structure of the apparent world, the formation of thought, the role of the energy that gives rise to the one and the other, and, beyond that, the energetic and creative power of which the world is born. By the method of reintegration, it allows to perceive the nature of the mental representations and the conscience and to arrive at the union with the subtle form of the being.

Yoga is one of the six schools (ṣaḍdarśana) of Vedic philosophy. The word "yoga" comes from Sanskrit, meaning is much broader than the commonly given definition of "union”.

Its Sanskrit root yuj means "harness, unite".

The word "yoga" has, in Sanskrit, the following meanings:

1) Hitching action;

2) Method of training horses;

3) Instructions for use, technique;

4) Spiritual discipline;

5) raja-yoga;

6) hatha-yoga;

7) State of union or unity of the subjective being with the Supreme.

So we see that yoga is the method, the means, and the goal.

Hatha Yoga

For a majority of Westerners, yoga comes down to Hatha Yoga. Yet not only is it not the only form of yoga, but even the form proposed in the West is far removed from what traditional Hatha Yoga is.

Indeed, Hatha-Yoga, traditionally, is not a form of gentle gymnastics but a spiritual path in its own right, moreover a steep and dangerous path reserved for an elite of individuals ready to burn the stages of Realization .

The term "haṭha" means force, violence. From a symbolic point of view, it also expresses the happy meeting of opposites, found in the praṇava, the sacred syllable om (the lunar crescent hosting the solar point).

From a technical point of view, Hatha-Yoga is a discipline of harmonization and development of the psychological (concentration, serenity) and bodily (power and flexibility) faculties pushed to their perfection.

The term yoga means "union" in Sanskrit. This ancestral practice originating in India preaches the union of the body and the spirit and the union of the individual soul (ours) and the universal soul (the Creator). This practice was originally transmitted from teacher to student.

THE DIFFERENT COUNTRIES OF YOGA

Yoga was practiced by Egyptians, Buddhists, Tibetans and of course Indians. In Europe Yoga appeared much later.

At the beginning of 20th century yoga reappears. In 1924, Sri Krishnamacharia founded a yoga school that would model Hatha Yoga as it is known in the West.

WHAT IS YOGA

Yoga has long been considered a series of slow exercises, primarily for women and retirees. These are accepted ideas. Yoga is for everyone except for special contraindications and you can:

To be dynamic and fast,

Exercise all muscles of the whole body.

Today, yoga tends to attract a wide audience. Alternative medicine and more relaxed lifestyle trends designed to limit stress and its adverse effects have made it possible to return noble letters to yoga.

Yoga is a Sanskrit word that encompasses several concepts.

From a modern and western perspective, yoga is considered a close activity of soft gymnastics, even if some modern practices are very dynamic.

It's not a sport, a gym, or a religion, but paradoxically it can be thought of as a set of them all. Yoga is actually a state of mind where a healthy heart and a healthy body hold hands.

It belongs to the Indian philosophy "astika" with five other orthodox schools and is based on the text of Patanjali, known as a yoga scripture.

Examples of yoga actions: relaxation, energy circulation, etc.

What you can do with yoga posture:

- Relax your body,
- Harmoniously develops muscle tissue throughout the body,
- Move the spine,
- In order to circulate energy at the chakra level,
- Relax your mind,
- Learn to breathe properly,
- Learn to concentrate

PHILOSOPHY OF YOGA

The primary preoccupation of Indian thought has always been the position of man in relation to the universe, and more precisely the duality of his condition: on the one hand the enslavement to physical and material conditions, and on the other hand part of the violent aspiration to exceed these conditions.

These two fundamental aspects of the human problem have oriented all research over the centuries, starting from the analysis of conditions of servitude, to go to the very elaborate methods of deconditioning. The Yoga-Sutra specifies this path: detachment, cessation of the activities of the mind, contentment.

The ultimate goal is the quest for harmony, unity of body and spirit, prevention or cessation of subtle changes in the mind (manas), sources of karma .

This harmony or state is inscribed in the present moment, and is potentially accessible to every human being.

Yoga is an inclusive philosophy, all beliefs, even religious or humanistic, can find their account. However, yoga is not a religion. The yoga proposing the union, the religious choices or not are respected. The main thing being the cessation of disturbances of the mind, it induces: respect for others, peace and non-violence.

PRINCIPLE OF YOGA

According to traditional Indian medicine, a healthy body and a healthy lifestyle are necessary for a good evolution of the soul and the spirit.

These exercises combining meditation, soft gymnastics, postures and breathing would release the psychophysical tensions accumulated in the chakras.

The chakras are centers of spiritual energy, located in the body, in correspondence with certain vital, mental and spiritual functions. There are usually seven from the lower end of the spine to the top of the skull. The liberation of the chakras would allow a better union of body and mind and better health for the practitioner.

In the West, yoga is considered a practice of well-being and relaxation. Although it is originally a spiritual concept, it is by no means a religious practice. It is therefore accessible to all, from the child to the adult, believing or not.

BENEFITS OF YOGA

According to the Indian tradition, yoga is a practice that affects the overall health of the individual. For Western doctors, its benefits are related to the well-being, relaxation or improvement of certain disorders. Yoga is recommended for:

- The treatment of stress and anxiety
- Improvement of lung capacity and respiratory disorders such as asthma
- Improvement of blood circulation
- The diabetes
- The treatment of musculoskeletal disorders

Physical exercises, postures (asanas) and sequences

- Give more flexibility;

- revitalize the internal organs, certain postures operating a gentle massage on our organs;
- revitalize the entire body by better circulating energy from head to toe;
- harmonize the musculature: yoga makes work muscles that otherwise would never be solicited by our daily activities;
- relax the spine;
- allow you to memorize a "choreography", a sequence, to develop your concentration;
- develop perseverance and endurance (through regular work of postures);
- strengthen the immune system and provide better protection against colds and other chronic diseases;
- relieve women who suffer from premenstrual syndrome ;
- Ensure a better longevity.

Respiratory exercise

- Improve the quality of our breathing by developing the ribcage (breathing becomes deeper);
- eliminate toxins and bacteria from the body;
- strengthen our vitality by circulating vital energy at the level of the chakras;
- improve blood circulation, decrease heart rate and blood pressure;
- improve the digestive functions;

- promote relaxation and better management of our stress;
- Improve the quality of sleep.

Exercises of concentration and meditation

- Improve our intellectual faculties;
- give us better mental clarity;
- eliminate parasitic thoughts and increase our joie de vivre;
- promote spiritual evolution;
- Allow for better self-control and greater openness to others.

Relaxation exercises

- Let us learn to relax;
- help us manage our stress;
- help us eliminate negative emotions
- Improve the quality of sleep.

TYPES OF YOGA

Yoga sessions are usually done in small groups on floor mats, once a week minimum. The practice is essentially based on the realization of postures (asana), the mastery of breath (pranayama), the learning of meditation techniques.

There are currently more than twenty different styles of yoga, including the following:

- The Hatha Yoga (the most practiced in France and in the West): Yoga balance body and mind.
- Prenatal yoga
- Bikram yoga : hot yoga
- Yoga nidra : the yoga of sleep
- Facial yoga
- The yoga of the fingers
- The yoga of sound
- Sexual yoga

THE DANGERS OF YOGA

Some yoga postures are discouraged or inaccessible to people with severe hip problems, multiple sclerosis or epileptic seizures.

Pregnant women will focus on prenatal yoga to benefit from appropriate exercises and postures. Finally, in the context of a recent surgical procedure (less than six months, the practice of yoga is strongly discouraged) If you have any doubt, ask the advice of your doctor.

HOW IS A YOGA SESSION

The course takes place in five successive phases, more or less long:

1. Relaxation: When you arrive at a yoga class, the first few minutes are devoted to relaxation. This relaxation allows one to leave one's worries aside and to

take a few minutes to allow oneself to empty oneself (pratyahara).

2. Respiratory exercises (pranayama): it is a question of observing one's respiratory rhythm and its changes. These exercises are essential for learning to control your breathing, focus better and listen less to the mind. Breath is very important in yoga to perform conscious postures, purify body and mind.

3. Posture preparation: this is a part devoted to the warm-up of the body by series of fluid postures and easy to access. The best known is that of the sun salutation (suryanamaskara), a succession of twelve postures.

4. Postures (asana): the postures are of course at the heart of the session. They are performed standing, lying, and sitting with progressive difficulty levels. It is essential to focus on your breathing and seek the letting go of meditation (dhyana).

For example, the position of the triangle is carried upright, legs apart. The student inhales deeply, raising his arms straight up in line with the shoulders. The hips pivot gently so that the right hand lands on the left foot. We maintain the pose, then after several breaths, we return to the initial position to redo the movement with the other arm. There are more than 80,000 different postures in yoga.

5. Integration, at the end of the session, with rest: at the end of a yoga session, the body needs a period of

respite and mental calm before resuming its usual activity. Lying down or sitting down, the student can relax one last time the muscles solicited during the practice and experience a calmer body and mind before going back to his daily life.

CHAPTER THREE

WHAT IS MEDITATION

Meditation is a practical mental and physical complementation and alternative medicine. There are many types, most of which come from traditions and religions. There are certain techniques used by people who practice meditation. These techniques include focused attention, specific body postures, and lack of attention to many reactions and distractions of unresponsiveness.

People around the world are practicing it for a variety of reasons. Some meditate as part of a long-standing culture and tradition in the family and society. Some people meditate to increase concentration and improve health. Useful for maintaining health and reducing the risk of many health problems

TYPES OF MEDITATION

When drawn from the concept of religion, it may involve the use of prayer beads or other objects that are considered sacred to a particular religion. Meditation can be practiced in a standing, sitting, or active manner, as is often the case with Buddhists. Physical fitness integrates its use with other exercises such as yoga.

This process is believed to be able to generate various forms of emotional states and promote the development of specific mental reflexes in the face of various environmental events such as compassion, anger and hatred. It has calming results that help inward self-awareness until pure and controlled consciousness is achieved.

One of the main benefits of practicing meditation is that it is safe and has never been associated with injury. One does not need any kind of equipment to meditate. All she needs is enough space. Therefore, doctors recommend this method for patients with stress-related disorders.

Can be practiced under the supervision of a doctor, health professional, yoga teacher or meditation, although you can practice with self-instruction, it is recommended that you first learn the technique under the guidance of a teacher or doctor, and then practice it yourself. There are various meditation and art schools that teach great meditation techniques such as Zen, Tibet, Transcendental, Tai Chi and Martial Arts.

Meditation 15-20 minutes a day is good and helps to relax the body, mind and soul. Research is underway to determine the various benefits of health meditation and its impact on daily life.

MEDITATION PRACTICE

Location: Quiet places are always suitable for meditation because they help minimize distractions.

Body posture: The position is determined according to the type of meditation. He may be sitting at the place, standing or lying down.

Focus: Different types of meditation focus on different things. During meditation, you can concentrate on the sense of mantras, objects, or breathing.

Open mind: While you are practicing meditation, distractions continue. It is important for the meditator not to lose concentration. You can simply observe your thoughts and slowly focus on your concentration. This can be time consuming, but regular practice can help you avoid the effects of distracting thoughts.

POSITIVE EFFECTS OF MEDITATION FOR HEALTH

Benefits of meditation for health include stress relief, blood pressure regulation, and anemia prevention.

RELIEVE STRESS

Starting with a 10 minute meditation session a day can help reduce your level of stress. Many people suffer from this condition, especially because of the lifestyles and challenges that exist in modern society. It may not be easy to notice the level of stress. Without precautions, it is possible to go to advanced stages that can lead to serious health problems. A good treatment for this condition is relaxation that is easily achieved by meditation. Researchers' findings suggest that transcendental meditation can reduce the risk of psychological distress and hypertension in young adults.

LOWER BLOOD PRESSURE

Meditation can also help manage blood pressure levels. Studies suggest that transcendental meditation practices are beneficial in lowering blood pressure in people at high risk for high blood pressure and psychological stress.

INSOMNIA CARE

Lack of sleep can have serious health consequences, including fatigue and lack of appetite. People with insomnia rely on sleeping pills to help them sleep. Some have even tried to stick to a regular sleep cycle, but the condition persists. Studies have been conducted to test the effect of meditation on sleep patterns, and the results suggest that regular practice of mindfulness meditation can help develop ways of working with nocturnal symptoms and the consequences of waking up. Chronic insomnia.

PREVENTS ACUTE RESPIRATORY INFECTIONS

The benefits of meditation for health include reducing the risk of acute respiratory infections. The IRA caused by viruses and the flu is one of the common diseases that affect many people. Good health and a strong immune system can protect the body from the IRA. Exercise and meditation are some of the activities that have proven useful.

TREATS IRRITABLE BOWEL SYNDROME (IBS)

Mindfulness meditation training helps maintain good health and alleviate irritable bowel syndrome. A study of women with IBS suggests that it is effective in reducing the severity of IBS.

REDUCES ANXIETY

Meditation helps reduce anxiety. The results of a study suggest that meditation reduces anxiety, blood pressure and helps improve the quality of life.

INCREASES TOLERANCE TO PAIN

Meditation has been used as a therapy to increase tolerance to pain. A research study suggests that there was an increase in pain tolerance in people after meditation and that the pain ratings provided by the subjects also decreased significantly.

IMPROVE SEXUAL HEALTH

The inclusion of meditation is effective in sexual therapy to treat women with sexual arousal disorders. She also showed a tendency to improve depression scores in women who had a history of sexual abuse.

HELP WITH WEIGHT LOSS

So far, emotional eating is one of the factors that contribute significantly to the increase in obesity, both in adults and adolescents. This type of eating disorder causes a person to consume large amounts of food even though they are not hungry.

Uncontrollable stress, anxiety, boredom and sadness cause this disorder. The inclusion of meditation helps control weight loss and the conditions associated with a bad eating habit. Controlling the portions consumed directly translates into a reduction in overall body weight.

INCREASE MEMORY

Meditation cultivates and promotes mind vigilance, which is very important when it comes to the level of intelligence considered high or the appropriate percentage. There are different ways to improve a person's IQ, such as regular meditation. Meditation helps improve cognitive function and reduces psychological stress responses. It also helps to reduce the rate of forgetting.

TREATS CHRONIC FATIGUE SYNDROME (CFS)

CFS refers to severe fatigue that can be caused by inflammation of the nervous system or by the herpes virus. Meditation can also be helpful in reducing pain and treating anxiety and depression.

CHAPTER FOUR

YOGA AND CHAKRA: A GLOBAL APPROACH TO THE PERSON

Yoga is based on physical exercises, but allows a global well-being. Yoga circulates the energy of the body and rebalances the chakras.

The mind-body aspect is taken into account: it is the holistic approach. Indeed, to cure a physical problem is not enough if one does not know to define the cause: it is necessary to determine the why before considering the how, for example: a headache can be of purely organic nature (hormonal, hepatic, cervical or other) or be linked to a fear (the patient somatized at the idea of returning to work every Monday morning for example).

With the holistic approach, we consider that the person consists not only of a body, but also of a set of energy currents that interact with each other.

88,000 chakras in the body: energy centers

According to some ancestral Oriental texts, our body would be crossed by 88,000 chakras, corresponding to the localization of the nervous ganglia and endocrine glands.

Energy exchanges and chakras:

Chakras are also called energy centers. They represent specific places in our body through which energy exchanges take place: inside our body, between the physical body and the astral body, and between the inside and the outside.

Chakra: a round and swirling shape.

In Sanskrit, the chakra means a wheel or a disc: it is a center for receiving, assimilating and transmitting vital energy, both in the body and in our environment. It is mobile and looks like a whirlpool that turns on itself, more or less quickly.

A decrease of energy in a chakra corresponds to a slowdown of this one: if you do not restore your mobility, then there may be physical discomfort, conversely, physical discomfort can lead to energy slowing down in the chakra.

CHAKRA AND PSYCHOANALYSIS

The first comparisons between chakra and psychoanalytic data are due to Maryse Choisy and Charles Baudouin. The latter is interested in a correspondence between chakra and instances of personality that he extracts (among others) Freud, Jung. He also points out the close relationship of the Tantric and Teresian descriptions (the dwellings of the "castle of the soul").

There is a movement of thought between "Tantrism and Analytical Psychology", where both practitioners of analytic psychology inspired by or searching for meaning in Tantrism meet, as tantrika ("practitioners" of tantra) are inspired by or being in search of meaning in analytic psychology. Some work on kundalini, chakras , etc.

CHAKRA AND BUDDHISM

These models of tantric Hindu were taken with some adaptations in the Buddhist Tibetan and Shingon Japanese or Vajrayāna or five centers corresponding to the five elements and five Buddhas Dhyanis are often described 9. More generally, in Buddhism, the wheel is as well used to symbolize the Buddha, the Dharma and notions of power.

The chakra is also, in Buddhist iconography, the halo or halo that accompanies the representation of holy men, behind their head, the shirashchakra, their body, the prabhâvali, composed of flames, the jvâla.

Before the meeting of the Indian and Greek worlds introduced a figurative representation of the Buddha, it was represented only by a chakra, sometimes at the top of a column or loft, like the capital of Ashoka which became the 'emblem of India.

THE CHAKRAS AND THE AYURVEDIC METHOD

As in traditional Chinese medicine, Indian medicine called Ayurveda conceives the human body as a microcosm in which energy flows through the chakras. We also find in the body the five interacting elements: Water, Fire, Air, Earth and Ether, which determine your Dosha. Health results from a balance between these elements and a fluid circulation of energy. On the other hand, an imbalance or poor circulation of energy will affect health. All the art of the companion consists in restoring the phenomenon of self-regulation of the body and energy, in order to allow the patient to regain his natural balance, to put the body on the path of healing.

WHY BALANCING THE SACRED CHAKRA IS PARAMOUNT

The sacred chakra, located just below the navel, is often connected only to sexuality. This box does not correspond entirely to it. Of course it is the conductor of organs related to the genus: ovaries, uterus, etc ... But it also includes the emotional root of the whole body, bringing together 80% of unconscious thoughts. With a blocked sacred chakra, the symptoms accumulate: dysfunctional relationships, confusion, too full of emotions, etc. In balance, this chakra is a refuge area, ultra secure and active in the body. With this solid foundation, we can move forward in life with more energy and joy.

RECALL ON THE CHAKRAS

In Buddhist and Hindu traditions, the chakras "contain" the physical body, in an envelope. They function as a complete system, or each of the 7 elements must hold its place and its role. They are part of a whole. For this reason, if it is advisable to focus your attention on a single chakra that seems blocked, you should not isolate it, since it is part of a whole.

Ayurvedic medicine uses chakras to cure diseases, physical or mental. Their goal is to diagnose the state of a chakra and its behavior in relation to others. In case of imbalance, the symptoms are various. It is more than likely that the chakra that "stuck" is only a collateral victim of one of its neighbors.

If the chakra is overactive, which area of the body or mind has it chosen to dump its over-energy? If conversely he is under active, he will look elsewhere for what he lacks to try to work. He vampires then his neighboring chakras especially that of the solar plexus, full of vitality, an unbalanced chakra also changes our relationship to the world, we then seek to "vampirize" others to feed on their vitality.

The alignment of these mini vortices is therefore essential. Especially when it comes to the sacred chakra.

The sacred chakra, in the most secret privacy of the body:

The kundalini is the mythical snake wrapped around the spine along the chakras. He is the life force in every sense of the word. This snake finds its source, not in the root chakra, as one might suppose, since it is the first, but in the sacred chakra. That's why healing the balance of this chakra is a priority.

The sacred chakra, or Svadhisthana, is connected to the water element. It acts on the sexual organs, the small intestine. It balances sexuality, desire, creativity, and a form of self-esteem. According to Hindu and Buddhist traditions, when we find ourselves on the right path, it radiates, brings life. If it is blocked, an emotional instability sets in, with clear tendencies to big anger "from nowhere".

On a physical level, urinary disorders, kidney problems and lower back pain can occur. Many yogis associate this chakra with the notion of intimate territory, because almost all our unconscious thoughts are formed there. We join the popular belief that a urinary infection is due to a sense of threat from its intimate territory.

On the path of the chakras between them, as soon as the root chakra is responsible for us to survive with the primary needs, it is the turn of the sacred chakra to complete the puzzle. It brings joy of living, pleasure without guilt. If he is strong, then we know that we have a safe inner refuge. We can live as pleasantly as possible. Its color is orange, a mixture of red (root chakra) and yellow (solar plexus chakra). This color is linked to enthusiasm, to vitality. She can erase sullen moods.

The energy of the sacred chakra is vital and joyful.

The quality of our love relationships is deeply linked with this sacred chakra. This also applies to the value we give to moments of relaxation and pleasure. Without falling into an unlimited hedonism, one can however choose to take time to practice what gives us pleasure.

SIGNS OF A CHAKRA UNDER ACTIVE:

You operate in a comfort zone that leaves little room for novelty.

You do not play anymore because you have more important things to do

Your creativity is buried under a down-to-earth list (like libido)

You have recurrent urinary tract infections, or lower back pain

Everything is planned. Spontaneity has no place.

Conversely, the signs of a sacred chakra too active:

Looking for pleasure above all, like an addiction

The unknown attracts you like a magnet: a new playground

You leave behind the vital needs to play the burnt head.

You multiply conquests on the Internet, in real life, or both.

You can also do our test here to find out how your sacred chakra is

HOW TO RE-BALANCE YOUR SACRED CHAKRA?

Meditation is the royal way of balance. It may seem paradoxical, but the more our life is active, filled with work, appointments, constraints, more meditation is essential. Sit and do nothing but visualize your energy centers shine with the right colors should be a priority in our world that runs from madness to follies.

The mantra (see our article on mantras here) VAM is the sacred chakra. It is this sound that will harmonize this energy center.

All yoga postures that open the hips (like the butterfly) are also perfect for opening this chakra.

Reconnecting with your inner child, if the chakra is active, will restart it. It's time to put the music out loud, grab a remote (and decide that it's a micro star of the song) and start dancing, jumping, and singing thoroughly.

On the lithotherapy side, the balance of the sacred chakra is delicate. The 80% of unconscious thoughts that sit in this energy center must be handled gently. Do all the orange stones resonate with this chakra? Not necessarily! Color is not everything. There is also the energy of the stone that will have to give the "the".

We chose the carnelian for our balance jewel of the sacred chakra (made in France with love), but not only. Smoked quartz will "defuse" repetitive patterns to take a new breath.

MYSTIC VISION OF THE CHAKRAS

The chakras come from a system of philosophical beliefs derived from Hinduism. The first texts that speak about it are written in Sanskrit. For people adhering to these beliefs, they have a physical and physiological reality in the same way as other organs, even if this physics is, in their design, much more subtle. In occultism, it is asserted that clairvoyance would see them as centers of light and energy.

Researchers called "independent" sought to confirm the existence of these points and give an explanation for their operation. Many people - according to some thousands - say they have the ability to touch and /or see them.

Those who examine the chakras describe them as living organs. Their function would be the regulation of "energy" between the different parts of the body, and between the body, the earth and the universe. Subject to the health hazards of the individual, they have symptoms of rigidity or subsidence, congestion or loss of vitality. They would communicate with each other and be able to compensate each other. Conversely, an action of "energy harmonization" (acupuncture type, even if it does not work directly on the chakras) would affect the health of the individual.

In addition, the chakras would correspond to plexuses and glands, which mean that their locations would have a proven function in the biology and even the psyche of the individual. But physiology, in the current state of knowledge, does not need to resort to the notion of chakra to explain the phenomena observed.

In esotericism, the manipūra-chakra would be located at the solar plexus, so it would have a role in digestion. As for the sahasrâra-chakra, it is located at the level of the pineal gland, which secretes melatonin, hormone related to sleep. But in occultism it is taught that it is the chakra in its subtle dimension that would regulate the plexus and the corresponding gland, and therefore gradually regulates and harmonizes the psyche of the human. If, for example, the hormone of the pineal gland is secreted in an adequate amount, it would be a harmonious chakra, and the individual would then have a regenerative sleep.

The scientist will say that it is thanks to the secretion of melatonin, the occultist will say that it is the opening of the sahasrâra-chakra that offers a refreshing sleep (see Wikipedia articles Melatonin, Sleep).

Sri Swami Shivananda goes even further in his book Kundalini-yoga, where he describes the chakras 8 [insufficient source] as spiritual centers that can be activated 100% by the rise of Kundalini. Each chakra would be depository of sleeping secret powers. The activated melahadhara-chakra would allow the yogi to levitate and purify himself from all sin. The vishuddha-chakra would activate the clairaudience. The âjñâ-chakra would keep the hidden power of clairvoyance in him. Finally activated, Sahasrâra would provide the supreme peace, the union with the cosmic being.

CHAPTER FIVE

YOGA: THE USE OF CONSCIOUS BREATHING

Breathing is essential in the practice of yoga. We breathe mechanically and unconsciously, absorbing the oxygen that is vital to us and releasing CO2. There are several ways to breathe:

- Abdominal breathing: is mostly done on the stomach,
- The costal breathing: is more at the level of the thorax,
- Clavicular breathing or upper breathing.

Yoga and other forms of wellness therapies use conscious breathing that has multiple beneficial effects on the body and mind.

PRANAYAMA: THE PRACTICE OF BREATHING IN YOGA

Yoga regards breathing as one of its basic principles.

Yoga exercises always combine breathing with practice. Each exercise is punctuated by breathing, which is done through the nose and not through the mouth.

One always starts with an exhalation to completely free the lungs from the excess air. Breathing helps to circulate the vital energy and therefore has all its importance in terms of energy balance.

Pranayama is a Sanskrit term:

"Prana" means energy,

"Ayama" refers to vitality.

YOGA: THE BENEFITS OF A GOOD BREATH

Relaxation is often practiced with conscious breathing, at the level of the belly: it is enough to lie down and breathe deeply by putting one's hands on the belly and concentrating on the inspiration and the exhale.

It is important to breathe "full lungs" and not superficially.

Proper breathing is essential for physical and mental health:

Yoga and breathing: the benefits on the physical plane

- Eliminates toxins from the body,

- Improves blood circulation,
- Slows the heart rate,
- Lowers blood pressure,
- Regenerates the body,
- Relaxes the body,
- Promotes healing

On the mental plane

- Makes the mind quieter and clearer,
- Allows to have a better self-confidence,
- Makes it easier to solve problems,
- Allows acquiring more concentration and memory.

On the emotional level: Allows you to free yourself from nervous tensions, etc

Different types of yoga breathing

There are several types of breaths that will often be taught during yoga classes. Among these breaths:

- Complete breathing: combines abdominal, costal and clavicular breathing and brings out the respiratory movement in the head
- Solar respiration
- clean breathing
- Alternate breathing, etc.

Yoga and breathing: a necessary learning

There is no point in doing yoga exercises by breathing badly or not enough.

Before starting to practice alone, it is essential to have had a good teacher. This one will correct our imperfections, as well from the point of view of the exercise as of the way to use our breathing.

For a person who breathes badly, practicing yoga will allow him to learn to be aware of his way of breathing.

CONSEQUENCES OF BAD BREATHING

When emotions overwhelm us or we are stressed or anxious, we take a bad breath, we have "shortness of breath". Bad breathing can affect our general condition, resulting in:

- Nervous and physical fatigue,
- Poor resistance to stress,
- Digestive problems,
- Palpitations,
- Lack of concentration, etc.

CONNECTION OF THE CHAKRAS

There are seven chakras and the five middle ones have kshetras. One can feel the seven chakras and one can also connect them in the context of the five chakras in the so-called microcosmic cycle or macrocosmic cycle.

Microcosmic circulation is called from the vertex of the forehead, throat, heart, abdomen, pubic area, genitals to the pelvic floor area and exhaling then on the sacrum, lumbar spine, thoracic spine, cervical spine, back of the head, apex.

One can associate with the exhalation: inhaling down the front; exhaling back high. In the Ujjayi meditation, you do it exactly the same way, in the microcosmic cycle or you can also do the macrocosmic cycle, you go down the front of the inhalation down deep into the earth, then perhaps stops the air and feels into the earth and on exhalation one then goes over the spine up to the sky and feels when stopping far into the sky. Breathing in from the sky down to the ground, you continue to feel the earth and exhale from the earth over the sushumna and the crest.

The energy channel did goes down from above is sometimes referred by and gladly to as Saraswati Nadi at Yoga Vidya. There are other nomenclatures where Saraswati Nadi stands for something else.

Sushumna is just the energy channel did goes from the back up. There is therefore the so-called sushumna activation breath, where you go from the front over the forehead center of the head and then the sushumna down to the muladhara chakra and exhale over the sushumna to the middle of the head over the forehead forward.

Some prefer to energize this breathing, some choose to focus on the Sahasrara chakra, and others love to create microcosmic or macrocosmic circulation later in the heart Or end or middle of the head completely Call into the silence to go.

THE CHAKRAS AND THEIR COLORS

Chakras are also called Lotus and can open or closed

In classical yoga the chakra colors correspond to the elements.

Thus, Muladhara Chakra is an earth element and therefore in the center Ocher yellow or as Yantra, as a symbol on ocher yellow square.

Svadhisthana has the lying crescent moon as Yantra and a silver crescent moon, as well as water silvery in the moonlight.

The color of the third chakra is the color of the fire, the symbol of the manipura chakra is the downward-pointing triangle.

Anahata Chakra has as its symbol the six-pointed blue star, as blue as the sky or blue as a symbol of the vastness. The six-pointed star consists of a triangle upwards and one downwards, so three spikes pointing down and three up, in blue, symbol of the air element.

Vishuddha Chakra is the color of ether and space, the space at night and so a purple, violet into the black.

Ajna Chakra is the chakra of the pure mind. The pure spirit has a brilliant white color and so is the radiant white, which contains colors in itself and yet beyond all colors, the Ajna Chakras.

Sahasrara Chakra is beyond all colors and contains all the colors in it.

In addition to their own colors, the chakras also have emanations and so there are the colors of the petals. Each chakra is also represented with different petals.

Muladhara Chakra, center ocher yellow, has red petals.

Svadhisthana Chakra, center silver also has red petals, but in a different color.

Manipura Chakra is orange in the center, the colors of the petals are shown in the writings as blue.

Anahata Chakra is blue inside, but the color of the petals is red, like something else red.

The color of the Vishuddha chakra is violet and the color of the petals is purple to blue.

Ajna Chakra is white inside and also the petals have white color.

You may be amazed by these color schemes, which have become popular in the West by a color correlation developed by a theosophist named Lead beater around the beginning of the 20th century, and he started from the rainbow. He associated Muladhara with red with red, Manipura with yellow, Anahata with green, Vishuddha with blue, Ajna with indigo, and Sahasrara with purple.

There is a certain correlation, the color that swings very slowly is red and the color that has the fastest frequency is purple and so he brought the seven colors of the rainbow into connection with the seven chakras.

Somehow this has become the esoteric and the new age Symbolism brought in, which is why many assume yoga. There are also people who say they can be linked together. Then the elements colors are the inner colors of the chakras and the aura colors are then the rainbow colors.

CHAKRAS AND THEIR ELEMENTS, ANIMALS AND ABILITIES

Activation of the heart chakra develops compassion, love, joy and connectedness

Chakras are represented in different ways, there are the yantras inside, the petals, there are aura colors. Then every chakra also means to an animal and therefore a god or goddess. Animal, god or goddess and thus Yantra, thus the symbol of the chakra, correspond to the element on the one hand, and the special abilities on the other hand.

Muladhara is the element of the earth, which means yellow elephant, symbol is the elephant, which stands for firmness, grounding and rest.

Second chakra, the water element is the lying crescent moon. Symbol is the source, silvery and chakra-animal is a form of crocodile fish, makara, symbol of fertility, for flow, for creativity , thus for purification and for healing .

The third chakra, Manipura Chakra, Fire Element, has as an animal the ram that stands for assertiveness, energy, charisma, courage , willpower , enthusiasm, and so readiness for the good cause.

The fourth chakra, anahata chakra, six-pointed blue star, symbol of heart energy, joy, compassion , chakra animal is the antelope, symbol of lightness , flexibility , openness , adaptability and the desire to connect with others.

The fifth chakra, Vishuddha Chakra, has a symbol of the vastness and the connectedness and communication.

Sixth Chakra, Ajnachakra is a symbol of the white circle, in the middle of which is the symbol for Om. The symbol can be in golden letters, but also in blue or red letters, with two petals left and right.

Thus, Ajna Chakra is the symbol of knowledge, Intellectual knowledge, that is the one side of the chakra. But also intuition and spiritual knowledge , this is the other side of the ajna chakra.

The seventh chakra is the Sahasrara Chakra, a lotus a thousand petals, beyond all colors. It stands for the opening of divine grace, which we want to open, grace flowing through us.

But it is also the pure enlightenment and the infinite consciousness. Thus, the seven chakras correspond to seven elements plus pure mind, plus pure consciousness. They correspond to seven fields of humanity, seven different abilities.

YOGA OF THE EYES: FIGHT AGAINST EYE STRAIN

Due to the multiplication of audiovisual, computer and other devices, our eyes tend to keep the same fixity for hours:

- Working on screen for long hours,
- Television,
- Use of the internet (social networks, private messages on emails, etc.) On computer, tablet and i-pod screens, etc.

This causes eyestrain and other eye conditions. It is difficult to do without these tools that are part of our daily lives, but there are some tips to avoid damaging our vision too early.

GENTLE EXERCISES FOR GENERAL RELAXATION

Eye yoga is a way to gently work the eyeballs. Doing a few minutes of yoga with your eyes several times a day is not only good for our vision but at the same time:

- gives us a break on the task in progress (even 5 minutes is enough): this allows us to relax by letting go of the problem of the moment,
- also allows us to do some breathing during the exercises, which gives us a boost of vitality and energy to resume our work in progress,
- We relax completely.

If the exercise is practiced just before going to bed, it can also put in a kind of bubble and facilitate sleep.

YOGA OF EYES: EXERCISES

Eye movements.

For example, look to the right, then look left, each time as far as possible on the right or on the left, without moving your head.

Repeat the exercise ten times.

You can then do the same type of exercise by looking up then down.

Targets to watch: Looking at a point (or object) in the distance and then returning to an object nearby, the visual adaptation is allowed to work smoothly.

Day-Night.

For example, put our eyes away from our hands and stay, eyes open, in the darkness, several minutes: this allows the eyes to rest from the light.

In this way the accommodation of the view is worked between light and darkness.

Yoga of the eyes: conditions to respect for good results.

During these yoga exercises, the correct attitude is as follows:

- To isolate yourself in a place where you will not be disturbed by the phone or the unexpected burst of a colleague,
- Rhythm the exercises that we always perform slowly with our breathing: become aware of the breathing and chase away any other disturbing thought,
- Not to be tense:
- Release all the muscles that are not part of the exercise, be in total relaxation,
- For example, when you turn your eyes to the right then to the left, you should not feel any tension in your neck, shoulders, or any other part of your body.

CHAPTER SIX

THE SEVEN PRINCIPLES CHAKRAS

ALL ABOUT RACINE CHAKRA

First chakra, the RACINE chakra located at the base of the spine, refers to everything related to the spine. Its localization near the sexual organs also makes it act on the genitals, the problems related to the bladder and the vital force. It helps the person to stabilize and take root.

Located at the base of the spine, the first chakra is called Muladhara in Sanskrit. This red wheel is built during the first 7 years of life. It captures the energies of the Earth to redistribute them in the body, especially in the feet, legs, sacrum, kidneys and the entire bone structure. Determining in our instincts of survival, the Racine chakra corresponds to our fundamental wounds, in particular that of the abandonment and rejection, born from the separation from the mother.

ALL ABOUT THE SACRED CHAKRA

Second chakra, the SACRÉ chakra, also related to the genitals and legs. It can also have an impact on the belly (physical stomach ache or fear, emotional aspect).

Located below the navel, the second chakra is called Svadisthana in Sanskrit. This orange colored wheel is built from 7 to 14 years old. It energizes the pelvis, lumbar, sexual organs and intestines. Determining our impulses and dependencies, testifying to our connection to our emotions and our pleasure, the Sacred chakra corresponds to the relation to the father, and to the acceptance of the law and authority. To allow then the construction of our own authority.

ALL ABOUT THE SOLAR CHAKRA

Third chakra, the chakra of the SOLAR PLEXUS, linked to the physical organs that are at this level: pancreas, liver, stomach. Emotionally, the solar plexus refers to power, control and also fear.

Located in the pit of the stomach, the third chakra is called Manipura in Sanskrit. This yellow wheel is built from 14 to 21 years old. It interacts with the diaphragm, the digestive system (stomach, back, faith ...) and with the muscles. It is the seat of emotions, undigested events, the relationship to the group, to others and to social life. The Solar Chakra allows the individual to take his place in the world to radiate his unique energy.

ALL ABOUT THE HEART CHAKRA

Fourth chakra, the HEART Chakra linked to the thymus, heart and lungs, from a physical point of view, on the emotional level, it is related to love.

Located in the hollow of the chest, the fourth chakra is called Anahata in Sanskrit. This green wheel is built from 21 to 28 years old. It influences the circulatory and respiratory systems, the heart of course and the thorax but also the immune system and the first 6 dorsals. The Heart Chakra allows self-love and rapport with others. Unique because central, it makes the bridge between the three lower chakras and the three upper chakras.

ALL ABOUT THE THROAT CHAKRA

Fifth chakra, the GORGE chakra linked to the problems related to the throat, but also to the thyroid and the vocal cords. It is also he who "governs" the arms, the hands. Emotionally, he governs "self-expression". When it is difficult to be heard or understood, when it is difficult to speak, etc., there is probably a blockage in this chakra.

Located at the base of the gorge, the fifth chakra is called Vishuda in Sanskrit. This sky blue wheel is built from 28 to 35 years old. It intervenes on the throat but also the cervical, the mouth, the arms and the lungs . The throat chakra is the link between personal reality and the outside world, and allows the expression of the individual.

ALL ABOUT THE FRONTAL CHAKRA

Sixth chakra, the THIRD EYE chakra linked to the pituitary, the eyebrows, the intellect and the sight of the third eye (intuition, dreams, sometimes and premonitions).

Located between the two eyebrows, the sixth chakra is called Ajna in Sanskrit. It corresponds to the third eye. This indigo blue wheel is built from 35 to 42 years old. It interacts with the face, eyes, nose, forehead and spinal cord. The third eye makes it possible to look beyond appearances to know the essence of things. He opens consciousness and intuition.

ALL ABOUT THE CORONAL CHAKRA

Seventh chakra, the CROWN chakra linked to the pineal gland, skull and spiritual consciousness.

Located above the skull, at the level of the fontanel, the seventh chakra is called Sahasrara in Sanskrit. This purple wheel is built from 42 to 49 years old. It interacts with the brain and the central nervous system. The last chakra is the one that connects us to our deep self and to the universal consciousness.

WHAT A STONE FOR CHAKRA

In lithotherapy, each stone, which embodies the skeleton of the Earth, diffuses a certain energetic quality. They thus resonate with the qualities of the different chakras, and help maintain the balance of these centers. Here is the list of stones associated with the seven main chakras:

The stones of the first chakra are Agathe, Ruby, Coral and Onyx.

The stones of the first chakra are Carnelian and Moonstone.

The stones of the third chakra are Amber and Citrine.

The stones of the fourth chakra are Emerald, Jade and Rose Quartz.

The stones of the fifth chakra are Turquoise and Aquamarine.

The stones of the sixth chakra are Lapis Lazuli and Sapphire.

The stones of the sixth chakra are Amethyst and Rock Crystal.

ENERGY TREATMENT AND CHAKRAS: SELF CARE

How to care, balance your chakras, get laid and receive energy to self-heal and regenerate, your body by defending against viruses, fatigue, nervousness, external aggression, cold etc. he gets tired and the more he tires, the more tired or sick you are.

The chakras are centers of energy in your body; they govern each of the organs, vital centers, emotions and the whole system of the body.

They are connected to each other. As a result, when a chakra is tired, the others take over and tire in turn. So that they do not get tired, it would be necessary to be happy much more often, the happiness, the joy, the positive energies rebalances the energetic system.

When you engage in Self-treatment, put your hands on your heart, think of something that filled you with love.

Call the energy: to do this, connect to Mother Mother Earth, visualize roots or a column of light that leaves your feet and connects to the heart of the earth. From the earth, the energy starts his journey and goes through your roots or your column of light, in your feet, then in your whole body.

Then visualize a pillar of light from your head to the farthest in the sky to connect to your guides, your higher self, God, strong, loving, and positive energy (put the name in you think).

Lie down (you can do it while sitting), breathe.

Remember that you are only a channel (like a garden hose), that it is not your energy that you use but that of the source (of the one you have called).

For mental treatment, stay about ten minutes with one hand on your crown chakra (top of the skull) and the other hand behind your neck. (If you have too many thoughts or need to see things clearly in a situation or in your life).

Put both hands on the first or the last chakra.

(Start with the crown chakra to bring down the energy or emotions or if you want to sleep next and through the root chakra to raise the energy to be in better shape for example.)

Ask to receive everything you need and the best for you.

Let the energy pass, simply, feel what is happening in your hands, in your body.

Visualize the energy you receive that mixes with yours all over your body, all your cells, eliminates the entire negative and brings you everything you need.

Let go, do not think.

Do as if you were falling asleep and if it is, it does not matter, you will have a treatment later.

Stay about five minutes on each chakra.

If you feel that the energy continues to pass is that you still need it, then you stay on this chakra longer.

If you feel that the energy does not pass anymore, it is because your body has received what it needs.

Go to the next chakra. So on for each chakra.

Once your treatment is complete, thank the energy mentally then blow or rub your hands to cut with energy.

Do you doubt your abilities? Act as if you had twenty years of experience, visualize how an experienced person would do and do the same.

7. The coronal chakra

This is the chakra at the top of the head.

It conditions consciousness, spirituality, relationships with guides, enlightenment, personal trans.

A dysfunction of this chakra leaves too much opening, which makes a dissolution on the subtle planes.

The person is then unable to make choices, has a tendency to disperse and cannot make sense of his life.

Once sufficiently open and dense, this chakra turns regularly and conditions the chakra of the forehead which is also that of the sense of the "I", the ego of the individual conscience.

Purple color

Mineral: amethyst

Endocrine gland: epiphysis or pineal gland

Body System: Upper Brain, Nervous System

6. The chakra of the forehead or chakra of the third eye

This chakra determines the activities of the mind, of thought, all visual perceptions (physical and subtle planes).

It is thanks to him that we have flashes of clairvoyance as well as visions of subtle energies, various plans of existence and spiritual guides.

It also has an influence on communication, especially verbal, and hearing.

Color: indigo

Minerals: azurite, sodalite

Function: intuition

Endocrine gland: pituitary gland (located below the hypothalamus), pituitary gland

Body System: Spine, Posterior Brain, Nose, Ears, Eyes, Endocrine System

5. The throat chakra

This is the chakra located at the neck and throat.

Its functions are connected between the head and the body. He determines the voice, the way, the creativity in the communications: writing, singing ... It has an action on the thyroid.

Stuck cervical vertebrae are often a sign of dysfunction to be heard or expressed.

Blue color

Minerals: lapis lazuli, chalcedony

Function: communication

Endocrine gland: thyroid and parathyroid

Body system: throat, arm, trachea, metabolism

4. The heart chakra

This is the chakra located between the two breasts. He determines love: how we love, how we receive love. Its root induces the discernment or the rigidity of not being able to know how to love, to protect oneself from loving. It has an action on the immune system.

Dorsal vertebrae stuck are often a sign of a dysfunction in the fluidity to love while respecting and respecting each other.

Color: green / pink

Minerals: aventurine, rose quartz

Function: love

Endocrine gland: the thymus

Body system: heart, liver, respiratory system, circulatory system and nervous system

3. The solar plexus chakra

This is the chakra located in the hollow of the stomach, under the floating ribs.

Its functions are to find and maintain our social position, it determines our place in relation to others. It also allows us to emit true yes and no, to assimilate external energies, to filter and not to take the emotions of others.

Energy assimilation capacity is related to the acidity of the stomach that allows us to dissolve food to make fuel for our body.

Yellow color

Minerals: topaz, citrine

Functions: will / emotions

Endocrine gland: pancreas

Body system: stomach, liver, spleen, muscles, digestive system

2. The sacred or sacral chakra

This is the chakra below the navel. It determines everything related to the symbolism of water in us, the functions of liquids (circulation, elimination ...) and also the deep emotions, the intrauterine life, our emotions related to life, the birth, the sensuality. It has an action on the genital system.

Orange color

Minerals: sardoine, carnelian

Functions: physical and sexual health

Endocrine glands: gonads

Body system: reproductive organs

1. The basic chakra or root

This is the chakra located at the perineum.

It determines all that concerns the relations to the earth, the matter, the concrete and the material, it is related to the symbolism of the earth in us.

Two of his four petals determine the eliminatory functions (defecation, urine).

The other two are related to material creativity (making children, for example) and pleasures.

This root chakra also contains a major part of our instincts (territory, reproduction, security).

It has a function of eliminating emotions when the woman has her period.

Red color

Mineral: red jasper

Functions: survival and prosperity

Endocrine glands: adrenal glands

Body system: kidneys, bladder, spine, skeleton, lymph

You can do this self-treatment every day and add a good smell, a pleasant light, a relaxing music.

CHAKRA: WHEN SHOULD ENERGY MEDICINE BE USED

Of course, energy medicine is not magic and can never be a substitute for a medical appointment! However, some "small boos" can benefit from an energy medicine session. Energy care, like yoga, has psychological, physical or existential indications:

- Sleep problems: insomnia, nightmares ...

- Stress
- Mood disorders: irritability, depression, sadness ...
- Accompanying pre- and post-cancer treatments (eg chemotherapy),
- Preparation for childbirth and accompaniment of pregnancy,
- Chronic pain (in addition to treatment): fibromyalgia, headaches, back pain ...
- Mental preparation for exams,
- Sports preparation
- Impression of being "lost in his life"
- On the side of contraindications, little to report: energy care is "only" prohibited for people with a pacemaker and people with severe psychiatric disorders.

Most chakras are said to be secondary, but 7 of them are larger in volume. They are positioned on a straight vertical line on the center of our body, along the spine.

The primordial energy, called Kundalini, will flow from the 1st chakra to the 7th, from the base of the spine to the top of the skull.

5th chakra the GORGE chakra linked to the problems related to the throat, but also to the thyroid and the vocal cords. It is also he who "governs" the arms, the hands. Emotionally, he governs "self-expression". When it is difficult to be heard or understood, when it is difficult to speak etc., there is probably a blockage in this chakra.

CHAPTER SEVEN

OPEN YOUR CHAKRAS

Your chakras are wheels of energy that distribute vitality in all parts of your body. This energy is drawn from your body, but also from outside, in your outer environment. Intermediaries between body and mind, your chakras connect the different elements that make up your whole being (biological, energetic, emotional and mental). A "closed" chakra is the sign of a withdrawal, a general malaise. So it is important to feel good, in harmony between your body and your mind, between you and the outside world, so you learn to "open" your chakras. This sheet gives you some ideas to follow in order to open your chakras.

According to the philosophy of India and yogis, the chakras, from first to last, represent the stages of evolution of the human being, physical, social and spiritual. They tell a kind of story, that of our growth.

It is therefore recommended, if you want to open all of your chakras, to start with the "base", the Chakra-Racine, and not to neglect or skip a step (a chakra):

Then perform each of the last exercises in each stage: "open the chakra" with mudrâ and sound, always starting with the first center, the Chakra-Racine.

However, you can only work on a specific chakra, or two, as needed:

In the evening, during a break, for lack of time or simply if you want a refreshing and light action, or wish to solve a problem belonging to the sphere of this chakra

The variants are infinite.

The fast balance of your 7 chakras

This exercise gives you more energy and makes you more intuitive, in a state of calm and well-being.

You are in a comfortable seat.

Inhale by focusing attention on the top of your head.

Exhale by focusing on your belly button.

Do this little meditation for a minute.

Hatha yoga for the 7 chakras

In hatha-yoga, it is interesting to know that Candle and Plow are "versatile" postures that cater to all chakras.

ZOOM ON THE CHAKRAS

In every human being, there are many chakras, but the 7 main ones, traditionally located on the middle line of the body, are the most known and the most used.

- Mûladhara (pronounced Mouladara): the "root", located at the perineum or pelvic floor.
- Swadhisthana (or Svadhisthana): located in the sacrum, spleen or navel, depending on the school.
- Manipura (pronounced Manipura) corresponding approximately to the "solar plexus" Western.
- Anahata : located in the heart region.
- Vishuddha (for French speakers) or Vishuddhi (for English speakers): located on the neck, by the throat.
- Ajna: the "third-eye", located between the eyebrows.
- Sahasrara: the "crown", corresponding to the fontanel, on the top of the skull.

WHY OPEN YOUR CHAKRAS

Your chakras are energy wheels that each turn at a different frequency. A wide variety of factors, including your own experience, shaped them. Depending on the response you gave to an event, synthesized by the famous “escape or attack” formula , you initiate a reaction model that will lead you to repeat the same response to similar events in the form of impulse.

The latter has repercussions on your chakra and results in a change in its speed of rotation. If this model of reaction continues, because you have not grasped the message or even noticed the inadequacy of your attitude, the chakra ends up not to resume its ideal rotation rate and becomes unbalanced. The nearby chakras will try to rebalance it, at the risk of destabilizing themselves, as in a chain reaction.

Rest assured, no one can respond in an ideal way to the events that life brings us to experience. Decisions made in the past have allowed you to survive such a situation, to maintain your physical, mental and emotional health. But your current reactions must not reproduce the patterns of the past, simply because they are out of date: life is constantly changing, you are evolving, and situations, apparently identical, require other answers.

THE IMPORTANCE OF WORK ON THE CHAKRAS

Working on the chakras teaches you to eliminate any routine that harms your integrity. It requires that you think about every detail, every gesture and weigh the pros and cons, to measure the scope. The work on the chakras is a constructive meditation and ... exciting!

Your body, physical activity, postures, gestures (mudras), allow you to become aware of your chakras and put you in touch with them. Some meditations to open the chakras use the hasta-mudrâ , which are special positions of the hands (hasta). The mudras have the power to send more energy to each chakra.

Your breathing, speech and singing, are major ways to open your chakras. In Hindu mysticism, each chakra vibrates to a sound (bijà) of its own.

Your other senses are also involved: sight, but also hearing, smell, taste, touch ... each of these has its own way of expressing its satisfaction, its frustration and /or to evoke souvenirs. A mandala is a kind of rosette that represents the cosmic universe in various simple geometric forms. You can attribute to your chakras particular colors, which are so many vibrations; however, depending on the school, these colors may not be the same.

Your suggestion has its importance: you can consider it, like sensory organs and their senses. It can also be seen as one of the means used by the body to communicate to the mind its strong desire for more well-being, less stress ... but in addition, it gives to the mind ideas about how to do it. What some people call "intuition".

An "underactive" chakra is obviously a closed chakra. It does not work at full speed and must be stimulated by exercises to open the chakras. An "over-active" chakra, on the contrary, tries to compensate for the weaknesses of a deficient chakra. It must not be solicited intensively under pain of aggravating its condition. Practice the exercises to open the chakras preferably on those that are closed. The symptoms you feel put you on the path.

Apart from this "chakra therapy", do not hesitate to concentrate daily on all your chakras. Just concentrating on them is enough to regulate their possibly abnormal rhythms. Gradually, you will feel more vital and have the power to change what you never thought you could change.

WHAT ARE THE SIGNS THAT A CHAKRA IS OPENING

For some people, when the chakras begin to open, they may feel a little tickling or buzzing at the place in question. The effects of openness are sometimes subtle and at other times they are obvious. It is important to know that if you do not feel "nothing", it does not mean that there is no opening. Get out of your mind and let yourself live.

Trust that the opening is present anyway. Confidence and state of mind are important keys to the process of awakening and improving health. The opening of a chakra can be done gently for a long period of time and other times it will be instantaneous.

The fear of certain individuals.

When a chakra is open, leave it open. There is no reason to close it later. Some say we have to close them to protect ourselves. But, in reality, the only thing that comes in if you want, is the light that is Love. Having open chakras is natural. That's how we were long ago, before the vibrations of the planet went down.

Fears, as in anything, are based on scary emotions (low vibrations, negative emotions, dark energies, etc.). Only then, the "bad energies" can reach you, if there are any. Thus, these "negative" energies are not the result of an open chakra.

On the other hand, it is important to notice that with any spiritual awakening, we have more responsibilities: the thoughts we choose, the manifestations, the energies we feed and the tools we use.

OPEN THE 1ST CHAKRA, CHAKRA-RACINE

Located in the genitals, Chakra-Racine is linked to the adrenal glands, kidneys and spine. It is the root of our "tree of life", the place of the cosmic and telluric forces that animate us. The red color is traditionally attributed to him.

Chakra-Racine is about feeling physically present and feeling welcome in all situations. It is the fundamental basis of the balance of body and mind.

With this chakra, we evoke the Kundalini (the energy of the snake), represented by a serpent wound on itself: the awakening of the Kundalini is part of the initiatory journey of the Yogi.

The state of Chakra-Racine and its symptoms.

Open: you have a solid foundation, you are stable and you feel safe. You are present here and now, connected to your physical body. You feel that you have enough territory and do not be wary of others.

Underactive: you tend to be fearful or nervous. You most often feel unwelcome. When your Chakra-Racine is too closed, you feel that your feet are no longer touching the ground; in other words, you "lose your footing"

Over-active: you can be too materialistic and greedy. Obsessed with the need for security, you resist change.

The Chakra-Racine is the most physical of the chakras.

Any physical activity that makes you aware of your body strengthens the Chakra-Racine. It can be:

Sports, walking, yoga, tai chi, martial arts but also cleaning, washing up, and cleaning your car.

Good to know: not all physical activities are of the same intensity.

According to the National Institute of Health:

Intensity very low / low: standing (ironing, cooking, practice of musical instrument ...) / walk (on foot, cleaning, sailing, golf (out of competition) ...

Average intensity: brisk walking (6 km / h), gardening, ballroom dancing, cycling, swimming (out of competition)...

High intensity: Hill walking, jogging, jumping rope, team sports, digging, relocating...

The important thing is not to exaggerate the practice of these activities in intensity and / or frequency: exhaustion is the worst thing.

THE CONTRACTION-ROOT

This very important gesture (called matla-bandha among the yogis), which should be performed naturally, consists in contracting strongly and upwards the muscle situated between the anus and the perineum. The contraction-root makes it possible to constitute a solid base for the body and to support firmly the internal organs. It blocks the energy at the base of the body and allows the vital energy (prana) to move upwards. In addition, it helps to tone the thighs and buttocks, associated with massage and walking!

In order to combat the tendency of the vital energy to submit to gravity, do a dozen "squeeze-release", whether you are sitting, standing or walking.

RESPIRATORY EXERCISES

To stimulate Chakra-Root , make the root contraction with each breath and release with each breath for a few minutes.

During respiratory exercises (prânayâma), the contraction-root is most often performed in full or empty lung retention. Be sure to keep the contraction steady and even, without forcing.

HATHA YOGA

The equilibrium postures of yoga, especially the Tree and the Eagle, require the placement of the contraction-root when they are held. By their rooting to the ground, foot of the support leg well flat on the ground, they are particularly

- Indicated to open the Chakra-Racine.
- Rooting

This exercise strengthens your connection with the earth.

You are standing, relaxed, parallel feet apart of the same width as your shoulders.

Place your hands forward to balance your balance.

Slightly bend your knees while advancing your pelvis but keeping the right bust.

Mark a brief pause to correct your balance as needed by spreading your weight over the entire surface of your 2 soles.

Then continue to lower your buttocks keeping the right bust. Go as low as you can without forcing. However, do not go over the horizontal for your thighs.

Hold a few minutes the position and your consciousness at the bottom of the column.

Come back slowly.

The balance of Chakra-Racine

This exercise allows you, or a friend, to balance Chakra-Root, in just 10 minutes. You will feel a great appeasement.

Raise an open hand, palm facing your chest, about 7 cm. Right hand or left hand, whatever.

If you are practicing for a friend, stand in front of him and point your palm open to his chest.

Circling counter-clockwise for 5 minutes.

Then circle in a clockwise direction for 3 minutes.

The recharge of Chakra-Racine

This exercise recharges your life force, at the most physical level. It stretches the spine and relieves tension in the lower back, lengthening it: your body is resting and recovering. Daily practice, especially after work, makes you feel "lighter".

You are lying on your back, with a thickness of 7.5 cm under the nape (magazine, cushion ...)

Place your feet flat with your knees up.

The hands rest on the pelvis (the pelvis, between hips and perineum), elbows as far apart as possible.

Stay about 20 minutes in this position: you eliminate the tension caused by these fixed postures that your body undergoes during the day.

The meditation "open the Chakra-Racine" with mudrâ and his

You are sitting in a comfortable position, one hand on each knee.

Touch the tips of the thumb and forefinger of each hand.

You will keep the mudrâ (jnana mudrâ) outfit throughout the exercise.

Concentrate on the Chakra-Racine (between the genitals and the anus).

Take a few deep breaths.

Then sing the Bijà LAM internally, on the exhale.

Do this as long as you want, with a calm breath.

OPEN THE 2ND CHAKRA, THE SACRED CENTER

Linked to Yin and Yang (Water and Fire), the Sacral Center or Chakra, located towards the sacrum, is connected to the functions of elimination of what encumbers our metabolism. It is related to the sex glands (sometimes called "Sexual Chakra"). The orange color, the Water Element and the sense of taste (sensory function) are attributed to it.

This energy center is about feeling. He controls the sexual energies and those of creation and gifts.

THE STATE OF THE SACRED CENTER AND ITS SYMPTOMS

Open: your feelings flow freely and are expressed without overexcitement. You can be passionate and alive and have no problem with your sexuality.

Underactive: you tend to be stiff or have an expressionless face. You are not very open to others because you are subject to fears, sentimentality, feelings of guilt. You may experience an excessive need for cleanliness.

Over-active: you tend to be aggressive, irascible. You feel emotionally attached to people. You can be very focused on pleasures and sexuality.

The vitality of the Sacred Center

By internalizing your energy, listening to your inner voice, you spread the influences of others, eliminate sacrifices, renunciations, as much as possible: paint, write a poem, keep a journal, visit a friend, go shopping, buy a magazine No matter, the more you enjoy yourself - healthy joy - the more you open your sacred Center.

To increase energy in the Sacred Center, create an animated meditation that combines movement and thought.

Swim slowly while maintaining an affirmation in your mind.

Take a stroll in the open air and empty your mind of all thought to feel in the present moment.

Do the same on bike, skates, skiing, playing tennis ... etc.

The "Butterfly" for the Sacred Center

The opening sitting posture called Butterfly (or Limited Angle Baddha-konâsana) relaxes the joints of the hips, the sacrum and optimizes the reproductive functions. It softens the knees and ankles, stretches the inner thighs and relieves tension. The small beats of the butterfly allow, between two sitting postures that solicit the groin, the pelvis and the lower back, relax these moments.

You sit, legs joined in front of you, back straight.

Take the Posture of the Bouvier (Gorakshâsana): move towards you, with the help of your hands, your feet, plant against plant. Your heels are directed to the perineum, as close as possible.

If you can, open your soles up (optional).

Leave your hands on your feet and keep your back straight!

Open your knees to the ground, align them at the same height.

Eyes closed, swing your knees up and down, like a butterfly's wings, at a steady pace for about 1 minute.

Do not control your breath, let it go.

When you have gained a good base, add an elbow placement on your thighs always keeping your back straight.

If possible, turn the bottom of the feet upwards (optional)

Then place an opposition with the elbows and thighs: the elbows push to open the legs and, at the same time, the thighs contract to bring the knees towards each other.

During contraction, always keep your back straight and breathe normally.

This contraction on the adductors strengthens these muscles and allows gaining in elongation.

Variant

Inhale deeply, fill your lungs to the fullest and grow your spine.

Take a short break full lungs by contracting the perineum (matla-bandha).

Then exhale slowly and completely as you lower your knees further down.

Take a deep breath again.

Take short break full lungs by contracting the perineum.

Then exhale slowly and completely as you lower your knees further to the ground. And so on.

Exercise 3 times with the greatest gentleness.

The meditation "open the sacred center" with mudrâ and his

You are sitting in a comfortable position.

Put on your thighs your left hand and over it, your right hand.

Palms facing upwards, the fingers of the right hand are lodged in the hollow of the left palm. Lightly touch the tips of the thumbs.

You will keep the mudrâ (dhyâna mudrâ) outfit throughout the exercise.

Concentrate on the Chakra or Sacred Center (sacrum, lower back).

Take a few deep breaths.

Then sing the bijam VAM internally, on the expiration.

Do this as long as you want, with a calm breath.

OPEN THE 3RD CHAKRA, THE SOLAR PLEXUS REGION

Acupuncturists know that a person with a stomach problem tends to stoop, as if to protect his solar plexus from external aggressions. Each one of us has also been able to note that when we have an emotional shock, we often bring the hand to the solar plexus: it is there that "it blocks". Stomach and nervous system are of the same family, itself related to the solar plexus. The yellow color is traditionally attributed to him.

The solar plexus chakra is about affirmation in a group. It is the door of emotional energies, the center of the unconscious and the personality.

One of the most important functions of the Solar Plexus chakra is to direct and control the desires and impulses of the first two chakras (root and sacred) and consciously transform them into creative energies.

The state of the solar plexus and its symptoms

Open: you feel good about situations, have enough self-esteem. With healthy and satisfying relationships, because they are based on a strong sense of identity, people show you attention, kindness, respect.

Underactive: when you are under the influence or influence of others, the energy of this center weakens and you experience experiences that undermine the awareness of your own worth, lessening your confidence. You do not get what you want because you cannot appreciate yourself. You tend to be passive and undecided, suffer the negativity of people and are sometimes treated with contempt.

Over-active: you have a desire for domination with an exaggerated conception of prestige. You tend to avarice and selfishness. Probably aggressive, you have a sickly need to clean, buy

The solar plexus in nature

In nature, the golden light of the sun corresponds to the light, of course, but also to the heat and energy of the Solar Plexus chakra. The adjective solar comes from the form "in sun" of this plexus; by analogy and according to the theory called "signatures", it was deduced that the solar plexus could have luminous, warm, energetic virtues. When you open up to the influence of the Solar Plexus chakra, its abilities are stimulated in you.

The following natural mandalas make you aware of how the inner experience can be a harmonious movement of orderly and sensible activities, radiating outward, in joy and beauty.

Observe a field of rapeseed or ripe wheat, in which the sun and its luminous strength are reflected.

In the middle of sunflowers, guess natural drawings turn spiral and in their petals, see golden lights radiate outward.

UNLOCKING THE SOLAR PLEXUS

There is a link between psychic states and physical states. Sadness, for example, acts on the sympathetic pathways which, with their vasoconstrictor role, begin to contract the arterial system, which hinders the circulation of blood and, consequently, digestion, respiration, etc. You feel compressed, poor, abandoned.

FOOT REFLEXOLOGY

"Solar plexus" is an ancient denomination for the neurovegetative center (consisting of nerves and related to the vegetative system or autonomic nervous system) located in the abdomen, between the stomach and the spine.

In correspondence on the sole of the foot, the reflex point of the solar plexus is situated on the median line starting from the middle toe at the place which begins to widen on the side of the big toe (about 2 / 3 of the height of the foot starting from the heel). To release all accumulated tensions:

Use strong pressure on this point with the seam of the folded index finger for 15 seconds.

Do the same thing on the other foot.

An impression of inner calm is felt in the majority of cases.

SOLAR PLEXUS RECHARGE

As the Solar Plexus is the reservoir of forces, when you feel a fear or a shock, immediately you are " emptied of your strength ", your legs no longer support you, your hands are shaking, your head is empty ... Your Solar Plexus has exhausted his strength.

But the Solar Plexus can fill up again! To allow a healthy dilation, call Joy, Love, strive for positive thoughts.

Tree energies

A good exercise to recharge energy

You are against a big tree.

Put your right hand on the solar plexus, palm on the body.

Put your left hand, also at the level of the solar plexus, behind you in contact with the back, palm against the tree.

Concentrate on the tree and ask it to give you some of its energies: you receive them by the left hand and you pour them by the right hand into your solar plexus.

Stay a while to feel the energies that flow between you and the tree. It's a kind of energy transfusion.

The meditation "open the Solar Plexus" with mudrâ and his

You are sitting in a comfortable position.

Place your hands on the stomach with your fingers pointed in front of you.

Put the fingertips of both hands in contact.

Cross the thumbs on the top.

It is important to stretch and keep your fingers tight and tight.

You will keep the mudrâ held throughout the exercise.

Concentrate on the Solar Plexus (a little above the navel).

Take a few deep breaths.

Then sing the bijra RAM internally, on the expiration.

Do this as long as you want, with a calm breath.

OPEN THE 4TH CHAKRA, HEART REGION

The heart chakra is linked to the heart organ, to the blood circulation. It is traditionally attributed to the color green, but also the rose.

The heart chakra is about kindness, the love of all beings, of all nature: universal and unconditional love. The energy emitted by this chakra multiplies your intervention possibilities a hundredfold.

The Heart Chakra is the center of the seven main Energy Centers. In him are found the three lower centers physical / psycho-emotional (root, sacred, solar plexus) and the three higher centers mental / spiritual (throat, third-eye, crown). It is at this level that you are given the opportunity to feel and share feelings. It is thanks to this chakra that you feel beauty, harmony, and that you feel affection.

THE STATE OF THE HEART CHAKRA AND ITS SYMPTOMS

Open: you are compassionate and friendly, you work to have harmonious relationships.

Under-active : You have a propensity to vulnerability and the ' hyper-sensitivity ; for fear of being rejected, disappointed or hurt, you lock yourself into a defensive attitude , which often goes hand in hand with an "inflated" ribcage betraying this protective shield against pain and attacks. A more pronounced blockage is signalized by indifference, a domineering and binding "love" that poses its conditions.

Over-active: you stifle people with your "love", which probably has selfish reasons, because riddled with demands, capricious; excessive needs to criticize, to possess, sign on the contrary of the coldness and a lack of heart even an imbalance and a depressed mood.

PRACTICES TO OPEN THE HEART CHAKRA

There are many exercises to open the Heart Chakra: yoga postures, affirmations, meditations, breathing ... Combine physical and spiritual practices and ensure a good balance of this center.

Hatha yoga

The back flexions (Cobra, half Camel, Camel, Fish), open the chest where the heart chakra is housed: integrate them into your yoga sessions especially if you want a more focused work on your heart chakra.

Centering meditation

This exercise brings your awareness directly to your Heart, the center of your body. Use it at any time of the day, wherever you are (at work, in a car stopped in a traffic jam, at home ...), to maintain or regain your serenity.

Choose a quiet place where you will not be disturbed.

Close your eyes.

Feel the breath of your breath going up and down in your body.

Place your hands on the heart.

Feel his beat, the force of life; feel it pump the blood to all parts of your body.

Keep your focus focused on the heart and its heartbeats.

If your mind goes astray, bring it back to the heart, the center of your emotional nature.

Breathe slowly and visualize a light or flame in the center of the heart.

Whatever the way, connect to this spark, perceive what it means to you.

Place some positive affirmations like "I feel good, I feel calm, in the present moment ..."

After a few minutes, exhale completely.

Open your eyes at the end of the expiration.

Breathe in the Heart Chakra

In case of stress, emotional problems or in an emergency, this breathing allows you to refocus quickly, to have a broader awareness of your difficulties.

Take 2 or 3 deep breaths.

On the following inspiration, imagine that a light coming down from the sky and another coming up from the earth, meet at the place where your heart is and form a ball of golden light.

At the expiration, which is done by the nose, this brilliant ball bursts in flooding your whole being and the surrounding world.

Do this until you have calmed down. But do not go over 3 repetitions.

The meditation "open the heart chakra" with mudrâ and his

You are sitting in a comfortable position, legs crossed.

Put your left hand on your left knee.

Touch the tips of the thumb and forefinger of the right hand you are wearing in front of the lowest side, fingers toward you.

You will keep the mudrâ held throughout the exercise.

Concentrate on the Heart Chakra (on the spine, at the heart).

Take a few deep breaths.

Then sing the bijā YAM internally, on the expiration.

Do this as long as you want, with a calm breath.

OPEN THE 5TH CHAKRA, THE CENTER OF THE THROAT

Located at the throat, the larynx, this chakra is intimately linked to our personal expression, our way of speaking, mimicry, the way to hold us. The blue color is traditionally attributed to him, as well as the Element Air: work breathing helps open the throat chakra.

The center of the Gorge concerns not only our oral expression (verbal communication), dependent on the breath, but also "self-expression ", our deep personality. The more we are fulfilled, exploiting our potential to the fullest, the throat chakra radiates.

THE CONDITION OF THE CENTER OF THE THROAT AND ITS SYMPTOMS

Open: you have no problem expressing yourself, you are able to show your weaknesses as your strengths. Your full and melodious voice can make you an artist. You can shut up and listen to others; your sincerity towards yourself and others manifests itself through your right attitude.

Underactive: You tend not to talk much because you have difficulty expressing yourself and are probably introverted. Your voice is trembling, sometimes with hoarseness or stuttering, your language, coarse or cold, your words, devoid of deep meaning. You have trouble thinking. But not telling the truth can block the throat chakra.

Over-active: You tend to talk too much, usually to dominate people and keep them at bay. On occasion, you are a bad listener who wants to question everything and always be right. Of arrogant nature, you search quarrel and tend to intrude everywhere.

Breathe for the center of the throat

Contraction of the throat and breathing Ujjayi

The attitude that you should most often adopt, which is to keep your chin down and to be aware of the slight stretching of the cervical vertebrae, prevents the mouth from breathing bad effects. The Jâlandhara-bandha ("contraction of the network") of yoga stretches the neck and spinal cord, producing subtle effects on the epiphysis (pineal gland) and pituitary gland (pituitary gland) and general relaxation. He accompanies the "noisy" breathing called Ujjayi.

The throat chakra is linked to a secondary and unrecognized center located at the back of the head, where it is attached to the body. All energy enters from behind the head. In a way, it is a "bridge" that connects the center of the Gorge with the first chakras (Sacred Center in particular) and the centers of the head (Third-eye in particular). This bridge must always remain open in order to allow the Energy to circulate; it's like the air we breathe.

The following exercise, combining the contraction of the throat with a breathing exercise, allows you to find your balance, in case you feel cramped in your personal space, out of ideas or in case of doubts.

Exhale while pressing the chin in the throat.

Your head flexes forward which stretches your neck. Feel this stretch.

Squeeze the top of the ribcage and bring the shoulders closer to each other.

The breathing must become snoring, always through the nose.

Continue to breathe deeply for a few minutes, continually looking at the back of your head.

Listening in the center of the Gorge

You can only listen to your "inner voice" without thinking of anything else. This innocuous exercise, which allows you to develop the throat chakra, teaches you to concentrate, to be in your listening, and promotes your creativity. This inner voice is sometimes called "voice of wisdom", or voice of "silence" because it is so fine and subtle. There is no word to express what this voice is.

You sit comfortably, sitting or lying, in a quiet and secluded place.

Take some deep but silent breaths.

As you continue to breathe quietly, try to hear an inner voice for a few minutes.

The first few times, you will not hear anything. Do not insist, do not go so far as to tire yourself and above all avoid any tension.

By continuing the exercise regularly, you will end up one day hearing your inner voice.

The vitality of the center of the Gorge

Practice whispered "ah" used by Alexander Technique.

Place the tip of the tongue against the lower teeth, lips slightly apart.

Inhale through the nose and relax the lower jaw to produce this sound.

Keep the jaw relaxed.

Practice this exercise 5 times in a row, which helps to release the tension in the pelvis (the pelvis, between hips and perineum) and the lower back, as well as in the throat.

Singing for the center of the Gorge

There are many ways to fill your throat chakra with energy. The best and most fun is singing. Singing brings joy to your heart.

Sing to open the Throat Chakra

This exercise stimulates the throat and ears. Practiced aloud, he relaxes the vocal cords and helps open the throat chakra.

You are sitting in a comfortable place where you will not be disturbed.

Take a few deep breaths. Inhale.

At the next expiration, start with vowel A, pronounced "AH"

You have your eyes open on the first half of the expiration period and then close on the second.

On a new expiration, repeat AH louder, in the same way: eyes open then closed.

Advice

At each end of expiration, note any tension in the face, jaw, throat: if necessary, move the jaw from one side to the other, repeatedly, before continuing.

Note any difference between the open and closed eyes, between the first emission of the vowel and the second, stronger.

Continue with the sound "E", in the same way as for the A: eyes open then closed, second emission stronger.

Then with the sound "I"

Then with the sound "O"

Then with the sound "U"

When all the vowels have been spoken, slowly emit the "AH" and "OH" sounds in an open or closed breath until they merge and give "OM"

Note the places in your body where this sound resonates: in the third eye, to the throat, in the region of the heart?

Now, let your throat escape spontaneously all the sounds you want.

Emit these sounds until your whole body buzzes.

If you sounded with open eyes, close them at the end of the exercise; if your eyes were closed, open them.

Stay still for a few moments to question your body and senses: how do you feel after exercise? Are the sounds in the room different now?

The meditation "open the center of the Gorge" with mudrâ and his

You are sitting in a comfortable position.

Cross your fingers inside your hands, except your thumbs.

Put the thumbs in contact, slightly raised at the top of the mudrâ .

You will keep the mudrâ held throughout the exercise.

Concentrate on the throat chakra (at the base of the throat).

Take a few deep breaths.

Then sing the Bijà HAM internally, on the exhale.

Do this as long as you want, with a calm breath.

OPEN THE 6TH CHAKRA, THE THIRD-EYE

This chakra, located on the forehead between the eyebrows, just above the root of the nose, is connected with the pituitary gland (pituitary) and the hypothalamus. The indigo color, a shade of intense dark blue, is in principle attributed to it, but as it is unknown to most people, violet is a frequent substitute. Perfumes are also associated with the Third-Eye.

Traditionally, the subtle center called Third-Eye is about insight and visualization. Seat of intuition, it allows access to spiritual currents, telepathy and other extra-sensory perceptions.

In direct relation with the two zones of psychic visualization located behind the ears and undergoing their actions, the Third Eye chakra influences them in turn, controlling the heads of the "energy serpents" that rise from the first chakra (Racine) exercising on them moderating virtues.

THE STATE OF THE THIRD EYE CHAKRA AND ITS SYMPTOMS

Open: you have a good intuition. You tend to dream awake (be careful in the good sense of the word).

Underactive: You are not good at thinking for yourself and tend to trust the opinions of authorities. Your thinking can be rigid and overly based on belief. A life without purpose, reduced activities, loss of memory and confusion are often related to an under-functioning of the Third-eye.

Over-active: a surplus of energy is extinguished by fanaticism, egocentrism, arrogance, excessive cerebral activity. You can live to an excess in a world of imagination, and in extreme cases, hallucinations are possible.

The vision with the Third Eye chakra

Ocular events

The "mental myopic" is blind to realities and possibilities beyond the field of his gaze. Paying attention only to immediate problems, he neglects to form plans, always postponing his plans. The "mental presbyope" does not see the opportunities under his eyes or at his fingertips. Dreamer, he directs his eyes on the future without taking into account the present. He wants to start from the top of the hill, rather than climb it step by step, but he has not yet understood that the only work we do from top to bottom is to dig a hole!

If we "see our life clearly through our spiritual eye," physical visual disturbances frequently accompany dysfunction of the Third Eye chakra. Thus, for example, difficulty in seeing nearby objects, presbyopia represents the fear of seeing what is present or in the very near future. Primarily affecting the elderly, it is surprisingly similar to the memory that follows the same process in these people, who remember less and less recent things but more and more clearly distant things.

Intuition

What you see is always an interpretation of your mind. You must train him to reconnect to your intuition and develop it. Many exercises help you.

Focus on the back of the head

With this exercise, gradually, your dreams will become clearer, and during the day, you will guess some events impossible to predict before.

Every evening at bedtime, focus on the occiput (cranial bones behind the head), the cerebellum, and the pineal gland (the epiphysis).

For a few seconds, try to feel like sparks.

Stop as soon as you feel this tension, as if you had touched a nerve center that makes your body vibrate.

Develop the third-eye

This exercise awakens your spiritual vision.

Imagine, with your "inner eye," you see the earth, the sky, the space, with the innumerable creatures that inhabit it.

Just look, as with your physical eyes.

So do a few minutes, without exceeding the fatigue due to possible tension.

Find a solution

To find the solution to one of your problems. This exercise, especially if you get the first positive results, even shy, has the other advantage of giving you more confidence in you to help you face the difficulties and adversities of life.

Go "see" inside your deepest self and question it.

Do this exercise several times a day for a few moments: do not worry by opting for a long session, which would have the detrimental effect of fatigue or discouragement.

The solution will eventually come to you one way or another (dream, thought ...)

Breathe for the Third Eye chakra

The so-called "yoguini" breathing is a noisy breathing that is characterized by a sound resembling the buzzing of bees. It is different from the breathing Ujjayi, another noisy breathing, in which you make the air pass through the throat (Vishuddha chakra) by constraining it (Jâlandhara-bandha). In Yogini breathing, you do not make the air pass through the throat, but, mentally, nostrils directly to the Third-eye (Ajna chakra). This peculiarity gives the yoguini breathing a power on the third eye, developing clairvoyance and will, in physical relation with the pituitary (pituitary gland).

You are sitting comfortably.

Take 2-3 deep breaths.

At the next inspiration, through the nostrils, drive the air by thought, from your nasal fossae to the location of the Third-eye, to the count of 6, for example.

Retain full lungs of the same duration as the inspiration, 6 according to the example (optional).

At expiration, of double duration of inspiration, or 12 according to the example, make it take the opposite way to the air, or of the Third-eye to the nostrils, while going down along the nasal fossae.

No retention empty lungs.

Do this breathing exercise 6-7 times.

The meditation "open the Third Eye chakra" with mudrâ and his

You are sitting in a comfortable position.

Put your hands in front of the lower part of your chest.

The adults are tensed up and their tips touch each other.

The other fingers are folded and touch at the 2nd phalanx.

The thumbs are pointed at you and their tips are touching.

You will keep the mudrâ (kalesvara mudrâ) outfit throughout the exercise.

Concentrate on the Third Eye chakra (on the forehead between the eyebrows).

Take a few deep breaths.

Then sing the bijah OM (or AUM) internally, on the expiration.

Do this as long as you want, with a calm breath.

OPEN THE 7TH CHAKRA, THE CROWN

Located at the top of the head (Crown), the Crown Chakra connects with the epiphysis gland (pineal) and our Spiritual Guide. The violet color, that of meditation and self-giving, is usually attributed to it, but there is also white, which is a synthesis of all colors.

The Crown chakra is about wisdom and the feeling of oneness with the world. Its main meaning is its ability to receive powerful spiritual energies. We become aware, at its "crowning" level, the action of all the other chakras, the concentration on the essential, the disappearance of the limitations and the union with our deep nature: the coronal chakra is considered as the seat of the supreme achievement of man.

Represented floating above the head in some ancient texts, or by the halo of the saints in popular Christian imagery, this energy center escapes the physical body and is not strictly speaking a chakra. It is nevertheless the culmination of the evolution of the first centers. The Crown is in correspondence with the first chakra (Racine), the fundamental basis of the balance of body and mind in relation to the faculty of attaining the goals we have set for ourselves.

THE STATE OF THE CROWN CHAKRA CHAKRA AND ITS SYMPTOMS

Open: you are unprejudiced and aware of the world, of yourself.

Underactive: You are not very aware of spirituality and your thinking is probably quite rigid. There is a lack of joy of life, of decision, of concrete realization.

Over-active: you over-intellectualize things and may be intoxicated with spirituality. Frustrated that you cannot handle these energies properly, your mental state becomes depressed and unpredictable. You try to repress these painful impressions in more activities to prove that you are indispensable. You are probably unaware of your bodily needs and are subject to very strong headaches; it is not unusual to get sick and be forced to rest.

THE DEVELOPMENT OF THE CROWN CHAKRA

The Crown Chakra can be likened to a telephone device by which we connect with the spiritual, the Divine or with God for believers. When we raise our thoughts in this way, this center wakes up.

There is no dedicated exercise to open the crown chakra, if not meditation, since work on the other centers, if properly undertaken, naturally follows its opening.

You can, however, stimulate the crown from time to time by repeatedly tapping the top of your skull with a sprinkling motion (the fingers joined at the beginning open up on the skull).

Too often, after a meditation, you immediately resume your activity, without respecting a few moments of silence. In this case, you cannot assimilate what you have felt, or take stock of the experience of your meditation, which greatly reduces the benefits of the exercise. After a yoga session, it is a rule to do a final relaxation to allow "integration" of the postures you just lived. It's the same with meditation.

So, after each meditation, stay awhile in silence and in a state of receptivity.

Access to spirituality works very regularly in the long term.

To develop the crown, make each day at the same time a short meditation, a prayer.

HATHA-YOGA FOR THE CROWN CHAKRA

All postures putting the top of the skull in contact with the ground, inverted postures (Pear or Posture on the Sirsâsana Head , Tripod or posture on the Kapalasana Skull , Clown Sir-bakâsana), as well as the posture of the Hare (Sasangâsana), are indicated to stimulate the crown, exerting on it a kind of massage.

The postures semi-inverted (upside down Dog Adho-mukha-Svanasana, for example) and the ocular revulsion (drishti) are also interesting to open the crown chakra.

Meditation "open the crown chakra" with mudrâ and his

You are sitting in a comfortable position, legs crossed. If it is accessible to you, the Lotus is particularly indicated.

Put your hands in front of the stomach.

Let the rings go up; their tips touch each other.

Cross the other fingers; the right thumb is on the left.

You will keep the mudrâ held throughout the exercise.

Concentrate on the crown chakra (above the head).

Take a few deep breaths.

Then sing the bijah NG internally, on the expiration.

So do some calm breaths.

Change the crossing of the legs and repeat the same number of breaths.

CHAPTER EIGHT

YOGA POSTURES TO BALANCE CHAKRA

The chakras, these energetic centers present along the spine, are worked in yoga using different postures. Each chakra is associated with a vibration, a color, one or more organs and a mantra. Asanas allow their balancing and alignment so that they are neither too open nor too closed.

Discover the top ten yoga positions to align your energy centers and move vital energy right through your body.

VRKSASANA, THE POSTURE OF THE TREE

How to combine yoga and opening chakras?

Regular practice will allow you to enjoy all the benefits of yoga.

TO WORK WHICH CHAKRA

The posture of the tree is associated with the root chakra (Muladhara), linked to the Earth. The goal of the posture is indeed to take root like a tree with the foot firmly anchored to the ground while rising to the sky. The posture therefore stimulates the energy center located at the coccyx, allowing the energy to circulate from the foot to the top of the spine.

How to do the posture?

To make the posture of the tree, we start another yoga pose, that of the mountain (Tadasana), standing, both feet firmly anchored in the ground with all the toes well posed. The gaze fixes a point far ahead.

Transfer your body weight to the right leg and then bend your left knee by lifting your leg.

Look for your balance and take your time before catching your left leg to place your left foot in the inside of your right thigh. If you are not flexible enough or lose balance, put your left foot on the knee or even the ankle. The important thing in this posture is balance.

Be careful to keep your hips at the same height and pelvis straight without arching your back. Raise your arms over your head or your solar plexus if you cannot.

Stay 30 seconds and do the same on the other leg.

DEVIASANA, THE GODDESS POSTURE OR THE POND DANCE

TO WORK WHICH ENERGY CENTER

The pelvis dance balances the sacred chakra (Svādhiṣṭhāna), located at the level of the sacrum, under the perineum. It is associated with sexual organs and consequently with sensuality, creativity and sexuality.

How to do the posture?

When standing with feet apart at least the width of the pelvis, flex your knees. Toes are turned out and hands are on the hips.

The coccyx is lowered, the pubis is raised.

By following your breath, swing your pelvis back and forth and from right to left, fluidly.

Hold the position eight to ten breaths.

UTKATASANA, THE POSTURE OF THE CHAIR

TO WORK WHICH CHAKRA

The posture of the chair allows working the chakra of the solar plexus (Manipura), located two fingers above the navel. It is associated with the digestive system.

How to do the posture?

Start the feet together by spreading the weight evenly in each foot.

Your arms are in front of you horizontally, spreading shoulder width apart. Open your shoulders well by lowering the shoulder blades.

Then raise your arms above your head and bend your knees to form a right angle. The weight stays on the heels. Remember to pull the chest up.

Stay in this position two full breaths before pushing the ground back to an inspiration.

BHUJANGASANA, THE COBRA POSTURE

How to achieve yoga positions?

Breathing exercises can help you relax gently.

TO WORK WHICH CHAKRA

The posture of the cobra balances the heart chakra (Anahata) , associated with the heart but also with the lungs, with the feelings of love and with empathy. Bhujanga means snake in Sanskrit.

How to do the posture?

Lie down on your mat with your hands flat on the ground, at your chest on each side. The legs are stretched backwards.

Lift your belly button and chest forward and up keeping your elbows tight against you on an exhale.

If you cannot fully reach out, it does not matter, do not force the risk of hurting your back.

Stay three breaths in the posture trying to go a little further each time (using only the back muscles). Then gently unwind the column and put yourself in the child's posture.

SETU BANDHA SARVANGASANA, THE HALF-BRIDGE

TO WORK WHICH ENERGY CENTER

The half-bridge allows balancing the chakra of the throat (Visuddha). It is associated with the thyroid gland and respiratory organs.

How to do the posture?

Put yourself on your back, knees bent. Your legs and feet should be parallel, wide of the width of your hips.

Try to bring your feet closer to your buttocks, so you can grab your ankles with your hands. On an inspiration, lift the hips, from the pubis rather than the belly button.

Be sure to open your clavicles. Stay in the three-breath position before slowly descending to the ground in the neutral position.

FRONT FLEXION IN SUKHASANA POSITION

How to warm up before practicing yoga?

Remember to stretch before doing certain postures.

TO WORK WHICH CHAKRA

This posture helps rebalance the sixth chakra (Ajna), the third eye (located between the eyebrows). It is associated with the eyes and nervous system, it is also the seat of intuition.

How to do the posture?

Sit cross-legged on your carpet. You can use a block or cushion to rise slightly.

Then bring your torso to the ground, trying to keep your back straight. If your back gets round at a certain point, it does not matter.

Place your forehead on the ground (or on a block if the ground is too low) and stay in the position for three or more breaths.

SAVASANA, THE POSTURE OF THE CORPSE

To work which energy point?

The posture of the corpse makes it possible to work the coronal chakra (Sahasrara). It is associated with the cerebral cortex and occupies an important place for intellectual activities, concentration and memory.

How to do the posture?

The posture of the corpse is a posture of relaxation, often done at the end of the session.

Lie on your back, on your carpet, with your palms turned towards the ceiling, your chin slightly tucked in and your feet loose.

Gradually release your whole body starting from the feet and going up to the top of the skull.

THE POSTURE OF THE CHILD (BALASANA) TO WORK HIS CHAKRAS

How to open a chakra?

The posture of the child is often realized in sequence of the posture of the cobra.

TO WORK WHICH CHAKRA

The posture of the child allows you to work on two chakras depending on the session you are planning: the root chakra and the third eye.

How to do the posture?

Start the four-legged posture on your carpet, knees apart from the width of the carpet and hands under your shoulders.

Position yourself so that your big toes touch each other. When exhaling, lower the hips towards the heels by leaning the bust forward and release the arms in front of you, palms towards the ground.

Relax by placing your forehead on the ground and stay in the position several breaths, time to relax.

THE POSTURE OF THE COW'S HEAD TO BALANCE ITS CHAKRAS

TO WORK WHICH CHAKRA

This posture is ideal for balancing the sacred chakra. It should not be done cold, do not forget to warm up before practicing it.

How to do the posture?

Sit with your legs outstretched on the floor in front of you. Grab your left leg to bend and sit on your left foot.

Then grab your right leg and place the right knee on the left knee. Hips should be on the ground and feet close to the hips. The upper thighs should touch the ground.

Raise your right arm and place your right hand in the top of your back by bending your elbow. The left arm bends backwards under the shoulder. Try to catch your hands by extending the neck and the column. The head is leaning against the left arm.

Take three deep breaths before leaving the position.

GREETINGS TO THE SUN TO DEVELOP YOUR CHAKRAS

TO WORK WHICH CHAKRA

The sun salutation makes it possible to develop the solar chakra linked to the pancreas and the digestive system. This sequence helps to awaken the body gently.

How to do the sequence?

Start with the posture of the mountain: while standing, your feet are joined. You stretch your arms to the ground, palms open forward and shoulders low.

Then go to Urdhva Hastasana (arms raised to the sky): on an inspiration, raise your arms above your head and look straight ahead. The next step is to lift your gaze to the sky, keeping your shoulders relaxed.

Finally on expiration, lean forward, knees bent and put your hands on the ground or on bricks if you do not touch the ground. Release the upper body and head completely.

HOW TO BALANCE CHAKRA

It is imperative that our seven chakras be aligned and continues to work in order to experience peace, happiness and vital health.

If these energy centers are out of balance, they can become anxious, fearful, depressed, or even sick.

So how do you keep the balance of the chakras?

Now this may be easier than you think, and here are five very easy ways to keep your chakra in line to prove it:

1. Spend time in nature.

Sitting on the grass or walking barefoot is a great way to feel more connected and absorb the natural healing energy. This also helps to keep you firm and bring more peace to your life.

Adding flowers and plants to your home can also have a positive effect.

2. Practice creative visualization.

Eliminating negative chatter is the first step to successful visualization. Once you have a clear mind, try to visualize an image of happiness and love.

For example, you can visualize the blessings of the flowers and hearts that open each chakra.

3. Breathe deeply.

Intentional breathing is one of the easiest and most effective ways to recover a chakra.

In order to make the chakra a natural and harmonious balance, every time you inhale, direct your breathing energy to the chakra. Exhale and let the consciousness settle down in the chakra.

4. Please wear the appropriate color.

Did you know that each of your chakras emits a different color? And does each color represent a specific vibration?

The red color represents the root chakra, orange-sacral chakra, yellow-sun plexus chakra, green or pink-heart chakra, blue-throat chakra, indigo or purple-third eye chakra, purple or white represents the crown chakra.

For example, if you want to balance the heart chakra, wear green or burn a pink candle.

5. Practice appreciation.

Now when you are in a state of appreciation, you will know that you will immediately increase your vibration frequency.

Raising vibration opens chakras and begins to attract more positive things in life, such as abundance, happiness, peace, and even better relationships!

And talking about relationships and showing more success ... there are really cool surprises for you that can help you become more liked, confident and respected.

Especially if you're naturally shy, it's scary to make friends and connect with people.

And unfortunately, this is not only a problem for your social and romantic life, but also for your career success.

CHAPTER NINE

THE MEANING OF THE CHAKRA STONES

All chakras are usually associated with a chakra stone. Here is a list to help you find your chakra stone according to the energy center you want to focus on.

Chakra Stones - Root: Blood Cylinder, Tiger Eye, Hematite, Fire Agate, Black Tourmaline

Chakra stones - sacred: Citrine, Carnelian, Moonstone, Coral

Chakra stones - solar plexus: Malachite, Calcite, Citrine, Topaz

Chakra Stones - Heart: Rose Quartz, Jade, Green Calcite, Green Tourmaline

Chakra-gorge stones: Lapis-lazuli, turquoise, aquamarine

Chakra Stones - Third Eye: Amethyst, Purple Fluorite, Black Obsidian

Chakra Stones - Crown: Selenite, Clear Quartz, Amethyst, Diamond stone chakras

LIST OF THE PRINCIPAL STONES OF THE CHAKRAS AND THEIR HEALING PROPERTIES

AGATE STONE (FIRE AGATE)

- Align the etheric body with the physical body
- Help keep your feet on the ground
- Intensifies passion and emotions
- Stimulates the root chakra
- Useful for diseases of the intestines and sexual organs

AMETHYST STONE

- Facilitates meditation
- Facilitates communication with guides and angles
- Helps to understand the root cause of an imbalance or disease
- Helps to reveal the self-destructive patterns of the ego
- Help those who do not feel part of the planet earth
- Used to heal addictive behavior patterns
- Help with clarity of mind

STONE CITRINE

- Increases creativity
- Increases clarity of thought

- Increases the power of will and manifestation
- Let's open up to the energy of the divine
- Help overcome difficulties and adversity
- Improves endurance and physical energy
- Supports the endocrine system and the good metabolism

PIERRE CARNELIAN

- Develops trust, courage, passion and power
- Help take action
- Helps overcome the fear of acting
- Helps to detoxify and purify the body of bad habits like alcohol or drugs.
- red carnelian stone

STONE CALCITE (ORANGE CALCITE)

- Brings solar energy to the body and the energy field
- Help with shyness or social phobias
- Can help overcome depression
- Good for the endocrine system and hormonal balance
- calcite stone

PIERRE DIAMANT

- Access to divine energies
- Facilitates connection with higher domains
- Promotes truth and vision
- Used to clear energy fields

- Can help eliminate the density in the emotional body
- Used as a support stone for other minerals
- diamond crystal

FLUORITE STONE

- Get rid of confusion and cluttered thoughts.
- Help to think clearly
- Structure and focus the incoherent energies
- Can remedy confusion, instability and dishonesty
- Balances brain chemistry
- Useful in case of dizziness and vertigo
- Strengthens bones and teeth
- Green Fluorite Stone

PIERRE JADE

- Harmonize and balance the heart chakra
- Help with emotional and physical well-being
- Attract abundance and prosperity
- Strengthen energy systems
- Red Jade Stone

PIERRE LAPIS-LAZULI

- Help discover his inner divine nature
- Activates the psychic centers in the third eye
- Clears the energy systems of the body
- Help connect with the gods
- Invokes divine inspiration
- Lapis lazuli stone

MOON STONE

- Used in meditation and regression of the past life
- Improves intuition
- Initiate the energy of kundalini.
- Promotes clairvoyance
- Creates patience and appropriate action
- Help sort out your emotions
- Can match the energy of the moons
- Helps stabilize women's cycles
- Real moonstone

OBSIDIAN STONE (BLACK OBSIDIAN)

- Eliminate negative energies
- Cleans the auric field
- Good for grounding
- Cleans negative emotional patterns
- Eliminates blockages in the meridian system

QUARTZ STONE (CLEAR QUARTZ)

- Boost energy
- Has a memory and is programmable
- Bring an increased spiritual awareness
- Open the chakras
- Develops consciousness
- Used to communicate with guides
- Promotes clarity
- Amplifies psychic abilities
- Stimulates the nervous system

- Growth of hair and nails

QUARTZ STONE (PINK QUARTZ)

- Heals the heart
- Wake up trust
- Relieve tension and stress
- Dispel fear and suspicion
- Calm the mind
- Helps to release anxiety, fear, anxiety and past emotional trauma
- Helps to balance the physical heart
- Rose quartz in natural stone

SELENITE STONE

- Open and activate the third eye, the chakra of the crown and the star of souls.
- Cleans the auric field
- Unlock cluttered energies
- Increases awareness on higher levels
- Encourages to move forward in life
- Helps eliminate stagnation

STONE TIGER EYE

- Stimulates the chakras of roots, sex and solar plexus
- Help take effective action
- Activate the intellect and sharpen the logic
- Energize the body
- Teaches the balance between polarities

- Promotes general vitality
- Strengthens the endocrine system
- Eye of tiger

TOURMALINE STONE (BLACK TOURMALINE)

- Used for psychic protection
- Clears the auric field
- Helps regulate the body's electrical and energy systems
- Helps to disengage from obsessive and compulsive behaviors
- Helps purify the body of toxins
- Supports the cleaning of heavy metals
- Black tourmaline stone

TURQUOISE STONE

- Protection against evil
- Increase wealth
- Stimulates the chakra of the throat
- Helps balance mood and emotions
- Strengthens emotional intelligence
- Promotes self-forgiveness, self-acceptance and the release of regrets
- Helps to oxygenate the blood
- Increase prana
- Natural turquoise stone

HOW DO THE HEALING STONES WORK

Chakra stones or chakra bracelets are used to activate, balance or amplify chakra energy. Crystal healing is based on the belief that stones or crystals have a natural healing frequency that can be activated to contribute to the movement or balance of energy around them. In the case of chakra stones, the vibratory signature of each crystal corresponds or resonates with specific energy centers.

You can use intention and intuition to activate the healing power of stones. Active imagination or visualizations can help access the space in which you can use stones or crystals in combination with healing the chakras. Feel free to check out this pearl bracelet online shop.

Energy is channeled and amplified through the crystal. It then affects or resonates with the vibration or frequency of the chakra you are focusing on.

HOW TO CHOOSE THE RIGHT CHAKRA STONE

First, you can check all the stones typically associated with each chakra. Note that chakras can have multiple stones and you will need to determine which one is best for you and under what circumstances.

You can also use your intuition or intuitive perception to choose your healing stone. To do this, use the intuitive sense or the most developed senses for you. You can look at the stones and see which ones are the most appropriate because of their brilliance. You can feel the energy of the stone by flying over the hand and feeling a tingling sensation or heat. Or you can simply know which one to choose when you need it.

CHAKRA STONE JEWELRY

If you wear a healing stone as a jewel, you may consider a stone that supports your overall energy or that corresponds to a specific intent. The crystal may have a physical healing purpose, reflect emotional or spiritual aspirations - or you may simply be attracted to a color that resonates with you that day. Remember that the power of the stone is increased by the clarity of your intention. So make sure you choose well.

We recommend using a type of string or mounting piece that does not interfere with the healing power of the stone. Neutral materials, such as thin strings, leather or pure metals, such as silver or gold, are good options.

Wearing chakra stone jewelry around your neck or as a bracelet is a statement for both yourself and others. Stones are powerful amplifiers and can radiate or attract energy inside and out by their natural qualities, their symbolic and cultural meanings, as well as the personal affinities you have with them.

USING STONES TO HEAL CHAKRAS

There are many ways to use chakra stones for healing. Once you have chosen the stone you want to use, place it near or on the body chakra. An extended position is easier to work with crystals. However, you can use a stone when you are standing or sitting by simply holding it in your hands or wearing it as a jewel on a pendant, in your pocket to keep it close to your body.

Concentrate on activating the resonance between the stone and your chakras with the power of your intention, meditation, or just relax knowing that you have the support of your chakra stone to harmonize the frequencies.

Do not forget to clean or reload your stones before and after use. For this, there are many methods: leave them under water or salt water for a while (pay attention to salt water because some crystals are sensitive), leave them under the sun or the moon the day or at night, smear them with sage, bury them in the soil for a long time for a more intense regeneration.

WHAT EFFECTS DO STONES WEAR ON CHAKRAS

Whether precious or semi-precious, stones have an indisputable effect on the chakras. You will see many therapists in alternative medicine use them to remove the shackles, the forms of crystallization or give back the free flow of energy from these centers of spiritual energy.

METHOD OF USING STONES TO OPEN THE CHAKRAS

The simplest method is to lie down while keeping your arms along your body, ideally in calm and silence. You can also light incense or candles. Then take the stones dedicated to each chakra and match them. Take the time to breathe and disconnect yourself from any constraints, just think of the stones. You will have a feeling of warmth, which will be neither more nor less than the contribution of stones in energy.

Breathe slowly while staying relaxed, remove any thoughts that would obscure your mind. In a feeling of fullness, you can then remove the stones by skirting them down. Once removed, take them and go clean them under a trickle of water (except lapis lazuli which is a very porous stone). You can also use the other stone purification methods and then re-energize them with the appropriate stone reloading methods. Newly ready, you can reuse them either as part of another session, or in the therapeutic setting.

Reloading stones, crystals and minerals

THE 8 MAIN CHAKRAS AND STONES, CRYSTALS AND MINERALS

MULADHARA

1st Chakra

Appellation: Root Chakra, Basic Chakra

Main colors: Red, Black

Location: Coccyx, base of the spine

Characteristics: Chakra of dynamism and survival force, the first chakra represents the bond of the mother earth. It is a source of strength, fighting spirit, well-being, but also security. It directly related to the bloodstream.

Matchstone: Smoked Crystal, Red Jasper, Obsidian, Bull's Eye, Garnet Ruby, Black Tourmaline.

SWADHISTHANA

2nd Chakra

Name: Sacred Chakra, Lumbar Chakra, Sex Chakra

Main colors: Orange

Location: Between the navel and sex

Features: Chakra of sexual activity, physical activity and artistic activity, Swadhisthana brings creativity in all these areas. It is directly related to the intestines, kidneys, bladder and ovaries.

Correspondence stones: Amber, Orange calcite, Carnelian, Sun stone, Imperial topaz.

MANIPURA

3rd Chakra

Name: Solar plexus chakra

Main colors: Yellow

Location: Between the abdomen and the solar plexus

Features: The 3rd chakra is the crossroads of all the energies of the human body. Manipura brings vital strength, the ability to achieve everything that is important to us. The latter brings us health and is directly related to the digestive system: the stomach, liver, spleen and pancreas.

Matchstone : Citrine, Yellow Jade, Suffer

ANAHATA

4th Chakra

Name: Chakra of the heart

Main colors: Pink, Green

Location: Chest, between the breasts

Characteristics: The heart chakra promotes love but also the communion of ideas in a general way. It is directly related to the lungs and the heart.

Stones correspondence: Stones matches: Green Aventurine, Emerald, Moraganite, Rose Quartz, Rhodochrosite, and Green Tourmaline Unakite

THYMUS

Chakra of Thymus

Name: Chakra of the karmic heart

Main colors: Turquoise

Location: Between Heart Chakra and Throat Chakra

Characteristics: Karmic Heart Chakra, Thymus records all the sufferings and misunderstandings of childhood and past lives. The Thymus chakra is directly related to anchoring wounds, immune system dysfunction, breathing and digestion.

Matchstone : Turquoise

VISHUDDHA

5th Chakra

Name: Chakra of the throat

Main colors: Blue green, Light blue

Location: Throat, Ears

Features: Chakra of communication, it promotes communication with others, whether for listening or speaking. This clairaudience chakra contributes to the proper functioning of the ears, the thyroid gland and the throat.

Correspondence stones: Sea Algae, Blue Chalcedony, Blue Calcite, Celestine, Blue Topaz, Turquoise.

AJNA

6th Chakra

Appellation: 3rd eye chakra, frontal chakra

Main colors: Dark Blue, Indigo Blue, Purple

Location: Between the eyes, between the eyebrows

Features: Command Chakra, the Ajna frontal chakra is a source of intuition and inner balance. This chakra is directly related to the nervous system and regulates all psychic commands. The latter is the center of consciousness.

Stones of correspondence: Azurite, Lapis-lazuli, Sapphire blue, Sodalite.

SAHASRARA

7th Chakra

Name: Coronal Chakra, Coronary Chakra, Crown Chakra

Main colors: White, Gold, Purple

Location: Skull Summit

Characteristics: Chakra of the mindfulness, it reinforces the good relation with the beyond and the divine being. It allows an excellent integration of the energies of the cosmos.

Stones match: Amethyst, Rock Crystal, and Quartz Milky.

CHAPTER TEN

HOW TO MEDITATE WELL ON THE SEVEN MAIN CHAKRAS

Meditation on the seven main chakras is a visualization exercise that allows you to harmonize, balance and control your chakras as well as energies to bring you into harmony with Mother Earth.

Begin the meditation upon waking, before you leave your bed and start your day because you are in a state of consciousness that is good conductor for listening to directives and directions whispered by the inner self.

TIPS BEFORE YOU START MEDITATION ON THE CHAKRAS

Chakra meditation will be your ally for achieving peace of mind

You breathe, yet, do you know exactly how your cardiovascular system works? You eat, but do you know how the digestive system works and its delicate chemistry? You think and manipulate concepts of unimaginable complexity without having to be a specialist in neurosurgery. Why do not you try to meditate on the chakras even if you do not have any special knowledge in this area?

Here are some tips we have to share before you start the chakra meditation.

MEDITATING ALWAYS STARTS WITH TESTS

Whether one is interested in Zen meditation, the Transcendental Meditation or any technique whatsoever, it is able to practice one learns. This is how we understand, because we live them. Meditation is always marked by attempts, attempts towards one direction and then corrections in another direction. As you go along, one refines one's perception of concepts.

It is necessary to practice before understanding and to understand. This is often confusing since you have to venture into completely unknown terrain. We find ourselves as a child, we must relearn, face fears, fears, the unknown. It is necessary to find a whole vocabulary, to make to coincide concepts with feelings, to correct constantly its trajectory.

CHAKRA MEDITATION IS NO EXCEPTION

The chakras intrigue and worry. So much is said about them that one always has the impression of missing out, not completely grasping what one is talking about. They are sometimes seen as caricatures, other times as things too ethereal to be seized. This feeling is logical, since it is necessary to practice to discover what it is and to be able to detach oneself from preconceptions. It is by forcing a bit of intuition and sensations that we advance.

Do not be uncomfortable with that. It is not a question of lying to oneself, but of paying attention to first, extremely fleeting sensations. Then, apparently, there will be stronger impressions, if only the perception that one has of them that is refined.

WHAT DO YOU NEED TO KNOW ABOUT THE CHAKRAS TO GET STARTED?

A priori, nothing more than a few lines in a guide to meditation on the chakras. Repeat the sessions, following the definite order, attaching yourself to feel the colors of your chakras and give them the one they should have. All this will seem extremely theoretical and abstract. Then will come a time when you will not need to force to get information, where you will be struck by the information.

PRACTICE MEDITATION ON THE CHAKRAS AS A COUE METHOD

No, it is not a question of being convinced that one feels something, but of attaching importance to what will be at first only very little detectable . This is so with all that is valuable, it must be conquered. The books that we prefer are those that are enriched with a deeper meaning at each reading, rarely those that give everything at first glance. Would you like to be as shallow? Be as easily detectable?

MEDITATION ON THE ROOT CHAKRA, FIRST CHAKRA

Visualize the red color and imagine a wheel, that of this red chakra which turns by deploying the energy of this color.

The root chakra deals with the affairs of the earth plane and the understanding of the physical plane, direct your consciousness so as to merge it with the emotional discharges of your life and your feelings of the moment.

The base chakra governs adrenaline responses to escape or attack. Use spinning as a soothing element on what you discover worrying about.

Blocking at the level of the root chakra indicates that an individual's feelings have been conditioned by the shame and contempt he feels for himself and the lack of understanding of his own functions. These feelings need to be clarified and balanced. In this state of equilibrium, communicate to the earth your confidence in it, it is the process of the return to the ground.

When you are angry meditation on the root chakra helps you to dispel it. If you have problems with your back or kidneys, meditate longer and spin the chakra faster because of its influence on the kidneys and back.

If you experience a drop in energy, visualize the adrenal glands and turn the red energy towards them, as the base chakra exteriorizes the adrenal glands. It is not necessary to know where they are, but it is necessary to know the existence of them.

When you balance your root chakra, which is the one that channels the energies of the human will, with the higher chakras, you are easier to live with. In other words, you feel better when you mix the red of the root chakra with the purple of the crown chakra.

MEDITATION ON THE SACRED CHAKRA, THE SECOND CHAKRA

After the root chakra, go to the second orange chakra located in the breeding area. This 2nd chakra governs the physical and emotional drives of creativity and sexuality. The second chakra is the center of our physical origin. It is from him that our creative energy flows, our attitudes towards sin and guilt. When we meditate on him, he helps us visualize and dilute these negative attitudes in his bright orange light. On a subliminal level, make sure that the red of the root chakra continues to spin, but the focal point is the orange color.

Meditation on the sacred chakra goes back thousands of years in Hindu traditions where the body is considered a temple dedicated to spiritualized sensuality. The partners do not imagine that their relationship will end at their death but that they will be united in divine communion for eternity, that they will be relived again physically when they make the decision to reincarnate.

This means that sexual gratification and immediate pleasure are not the goals sought by those who dominate their sexual activities, which today too often end in anger, pain and resentment.

Meditation on the second chakra is a way to face the fear of not being creative, therefore unproductive.

When you see the second chakra, use the image of a juicy orange, spin the juice and the orange color across the reproductive tract, watch how it cleans it of any conflicting feelings, confusion, worry, how it governs your intimate behavior and your creative relationships. .

It should be mentioned here that we meditate and visualize all, whether we call it that way or otherwise. When, for example, a sexual fantasy comes to us, we visualize it. If we visualize this fantasy to the point that it affects the body (orgasm), we can see that the power of the mind can actually affect the body. The same visualization process can also help heal the body.

The chakras centers spontaneously turn in their own color but we can visualize the acceleration of their rotation. It is not essential to "see" the colors you are turning, if you remember the "meaning" of these colors.

If you have trouble visualizing, for example, red, reinforces this visualization by remembering a bright red apple or a ruby or any red shape you like more. The chosen image is enough to inspire the reality of the color on which you want to meditate. With practice, color viewing becomes easier.

MEDITATION ON THE SOLAR PLEXUS CHAKRA, THE THIRD CHAKRA

It is important to balance the third chakra, or solar plexus chakra, especially when emotional acrobatics occur in your life. This chakra governs our attitudes towards personal power. It is that of the sensibility and the seat of the ego.

The biggest obstacle to our development and the balance of the third chakra is the ego. He is connected to the fear of losing something, someone, or a part of himself. From this fear arises the need to manipulate, brutalize and control people's lives in a devious way. When we succeed in harmonizing the third chakra, we love ourselves better, gain self-assurance, and therefore we are better able to break the negative attachments of the ego.

In relationships that provoke emotional disorders, personal power and the ego are always involved in what strikes our sensibilities. By visualizing and meditating on the yellow chakra of the solar plexus, directing the yellow color to bathe your plexus, you will manage to relax and “allow" anything to happen.

The calming effect requires a sunny yellow quality in which the vibration of the emotional disorder melts, whatever it is.

Bathing with yellow light the pancreas that regulates the functions of the liver, spleen, stomach and gallbladder helps to calm and relax the nervous system.

The balance of the third chakra is related to the way we use, abuse, misuse our personal power.

When we feel that the wheel of the third chakra turns in balance, that it is strengthened in the role that it plays in our emotional life, the effect is striking. Yellow is a solar color. The sun, our source of heat and power, makes us feel good. It lights our minds. We cannot do without its warm yellow light for a very long time.

Thanks to the power of visualization, it is possible to create an internal sensation of solar heat. Our sensitivity feels reassured by the acceptance of our personal power, this province governed by the solar plexus chakra. When this happens, the stomach, liver, gallbladder and spleen relax; vibrate at a more regular frequency, and our ego problems decrease in intensity.

By visualizing the orange, we bring out the creative and sexual energies of the second chakra in the sensitivity and personal power of the third chakra. If we color this balance of red, we root our understanding of the emotional balance restored in our physical relationships with the earth. This process helps to rid us of the fear and dilemma of

The whole panoply of physical and emotional impulses expressed through the seven chakras can therefore be modified, balanced and aligned by consciously playing with the vibrations of the rainbow colors. One can use one's body as an instrument. These colors are available to us at any time of our life. They operate and spin in harmony, whether we recognize it consciously or not.

Again, we are what we are aware of. And to be more aware of the value of chakras is to be more aware of one's own inner power. To be aware of one's inner power is to understand the potentiality of our external power. We can create what we want on the outside by recognizing the power hidden inside. The challenge of life is then to know how we create this external power and what we do with it when it comes to ours.

This leads us to the examination of the four upper chakras above the solar plexus.

MEDITATION ON THE CHAKRA OF THE HEART, THE FOURTH CHAKRA

As the fourth chakra governs the heart when we meditate and visualize its green color, we stimulate it so that it is more effective in its management of the feelings in love and that it also balances the endocrine and immune systems.

The radiation produced by the love drive can heal the whole body.

Meditation on the heart chakra promotes the process of self-love so that the love of others is facilitated.

The resulting assurance exudes a subtle vibration that is felt by family, friends, and employees in professional life. We receive from others what we have already seen and created in ourselves. Our internal security creates security for others. All this is elaborated in the heart center.

All that happens in our lives comes essentially from the heart, visualize the brilliant green of an emerald and remember that we give the earth the name of green planet. The vibration of the green is soothing and generates life. On Earth, there is greener than any other color because our planet is vibrant with life.

Try infusing the green of the heart chakra into the yellow of the solar plexus chakra before moving on to the red and orange chakras. You can play this therapy of colors in so many ways that the game becomes an adventure and you will feel different vibratory frequencies operate in harmony.

The colors of the clothes you choose to wear have a decisive influence on your consciousness during the day.

A bright green is a definitive position taken because of the frequency attached to it.

When we are red with anger or apprehension, we feel the symptoms of “attack or flight", the syndrome of the first chakra. If you are angry, wearing red only fuels it, unless you mix it with another color. It can be neutralized with green, because the vibrations of the heart help to calm the rabies.

MEDITATION ON THE CHAKRA OF THE THROAT, THE FIFTH CHAKRA

The fifth chakra, also known as the throat chakra, is the one we would all recognize and meditate on because it is the center through which we communicate, express and formulate judgments about others. It also reigns on the organs that convert the air we breathe into expression: the lungs, the vocal cords and the respiratory system.

Since it is the chakra of judgment and expression, when we meditate, it helps us radically to give up bad feelings against others.

In many ways, we often feel cut off from others by the rising rage born in our minds. They alienate us and only serve to feed the bad feelings. We cling to hatred, anger and anchoring. And these feelings chained us.

Anger gives us a dramatic role, ignites us, releases energy, and defines a relationship. It even connects us to the unconscious fear of what could fill the void if we free ourselves from it! But when we are able to give it up, relief overwhelms us and love also. And we find that love is the glue that makes everything stands, the way of communication of souls. These same judgments that made us reject by others are therefore understood and welcome because they carry a renewed and positive energy. We know best when to talk or to be quiet and how to do it more effectively. We anchored in a flow of love.

If you have a feeling of misunderstanding, meditate on the blue chakra throat to get rid of blockages that prevent me from being clear. When the misunderstanding is sexual, add the orange. If it is an emotional problem with your own personal power, mix yellow with blue.

The blockage of the chakra of the throat can be caused also by the fear to emit your own truth. Always wanting to please others by sacrificing your own expression of truth can create intense frustration in communication.

Whenever you are preparing to say some hard truth about someone, try to remember to visualize blue and mix it with a beautiful green from the heart before speaking.

In this way you save the inevitable karmic return of your hardness turned against me.

MEDITATION ON THE THIRD EYE CHAKRA, THE SIXTH CHAKRA

The sixth chakra, or third eye, or face chakra, located in a highly visible area behind the center of the forehead, controls how we present ourselves to the face of the world. If our features are tense with worry and anxiety, we can relax them by meditating on indigo color. It allows us to agree on our inner vision, our idealism and our imagination.

The third eye exteriorizing the pituitary gland, it governs a large part of the forebrain and the nervous system. He also governs all our comings and goings in our thoughts and visions. It is the center of the awakening of consciousness.

We can use the inner energy as we please. The choice of our thoughts determines external manifestations. With our third eye, we can arrange and orchestrate our inner divine energy.

Meditate on the third eye chakra when you want to manifest an aspect of yourself outside. The composition of colors and sensations of our lives is potentially unlimited.

MEDITATION ON THE CORONAL CHAKRA, THE SEVENTH CHAKRA

The vibration frequency of the seventh chakra is greater than that of all other chakras. The purple oscillates faster than any other color and rightly so because the crown chakra operates Divine final integration.

The higher we go, the better we can see where we are coming from. This applies to the physical as well as the spiritual sense.

Anger, seen from the chakra of the heart, gives way to understanding, hatred to love, possession to freedom. From this privileged outpost, we can more easily see the dark emotions of fear, depression, hatred, and so on. To compromise our energy and, finally, to make us sick.

The problems that had seemed colossal then become absurd, not that they have diminished in size, but because we have become larger than they.

In this new light, existence opens unlimited possibilities. We feel compassion for those who do not see it yet. We see each other in them, and we remember how difficult it was. Our behavior always depends on how we perceive ourselves in relation to the outside world.

It is said that when one experiences the violet flame one vibrates in perfect alignment with the strength of God existing in us.

If we feel the need to spiritualize one of the "lower" chakras and the emotions that correspond to it, it is advisable to integrate in our visualizations and our meditations the purple color, in order to infuse in the conscious its divine frequency. It is important not to focus only on the colors associated with the chakras, but also to incorporate the emotions associated with them that you wish to dispel.

The language of colors can heal, because healing is effected fundamentally by the successful alignment of the conscious with the spiritual centers.

Combine your chakras aligned and sanitized light frequencies of all colors and visualize above your head a bright white light. White light results from the combination of all light frequencies.

This white light that so many people describe for having seen it during their "out of their body" experiences is the infusion of all emotional frequencies. When its realization is perfect, it becomes the essence of God.

For this reason, when you surround yourself with a bubble of white light, you are, in essence, surrounded by the light of God, in which you are loved and protected and, in return, loving. And again, you become what you visualize, in the image of God.

CHAPTER ELEVEN

FREQUENTLY ASKED QUESTIONS

WHAT ARE OUR BODY CHAKRAS

It contains 7 chakras. Root chakra, sacral chakra, solar plexus chakra, chakra heart, throat chakra, third eye chakra, and finally crown chakra. The chakra is the center of seven mental powers contained within each human body

CAN YOU FEEL THE ROTATING CHAKRA

If the chakra is not rotating clockwise, health and well-being are in an optimal balance. When the chakra is clogged or not rotating

HOW CAN I BALANCE MY CHAKRAS MYSELF

If chakras are blocked, how do you adjust or maintain them?

Color; choose a color to wear based on your intuition

Food, you are trying to balance the same colors of chakras

Sound

Get in shape

Essential oil

Visualization

HOW DO YOU BALANCE THE CHAKRAS

Intentional breathing is one of the easiest and most effective ways to recover a chakra. In order to make the chakra a natural and harmonious balance, every time you inhale, direct your breathing energy to the chakra. Exhale and calm consciousness in the chakra.

WHAT ARE THE ESSENTIAL OILS SUITABLE FOR THE ROOT CHAKRA

Foot massage is a great way to balance the root chakra that adjusts the sense of ground and stability. Nutmeg activates the loose root chakra, while patchouli and vetiver calm down the overactive chakra. Choose a balanced essential oil such as bergamot to help maintain a root chakra that functions smoothly.

WHY IS THE CHAKRA BLOCKED

Chakras are blocked by negative energy that cannot be released from the body. It is the negative energy experienced as a response to traumatic life experiences and emotional challenges. Experience these negative energies and without the ability to release them, they can't stop us

WHICH CHAKRAS ARE RELATED TO SHAME

The solar plexus chakra (also known as Manipura or the third chakra) treats your willpower and is disturbed by shame. The solar plexus chakra is the most commonly blocked chakra and seems to be the cause of many complaints.

WHICH CHAKRA CAUSES EMOTIONS

Chakra 2: Sacrum

This chakra is related to emotion, creativity, sexual energy and flow.

HOW DO YOU ACTIVATE YOUR CHAKRAS

If you have a chakra open, understand that you don't have to try to make an overactive chakra. ...

Open the root chakra (red). ...

Open the sacral chakra (orange). ...

Open the navel chakra (yellow). ...

Open the heart chakra (green). ...

Open the throat chakra (light blue). ...

Open Third Eye Chakra (Indigo).

WHAT IMPACT DOES CHAKRA HAVE ON US

Chakra energy rotates in the clockwise direction and is drawn from the body to the field around us, and rotates counterclockwise and moves from the outside world to the body. Chakras exist in seven items of our body, and each of the seven chakras is associated with a different body organ and gland.

WHY IS THE CROWN CHAKRA TINGLING

Symptoms occur in the head (crown) and the entire spine. It may tingle on the forehead. The tingling sensation is related to the energy flowing through you. Whenever you feel a tingling in your head, it means that you are receiving.

HOW CAN I BALANCE CHAKRA AND CRYSTAL

There is a belief that chakras can be balanced using crystals. You can put the crystal on your body, wear it, or carry it.

Method 2 Put on the crystal

Rinse the crystal. ...

Relax and balance the chakra. ...

Place the crystal on the chakra. ...

Make the crystals work. ...

Remove the crystals.

IS THE CHAKRA RELIGIOUS

Prominent in the physiological practice of chakras, also spell chakras, Sanskrit chakras ("wheels"), one of several mental energy centers of the body, certain forms of Hinduism and Tantric Buddhist occultism

WILL REIKI CLEAR THE CHAKRA

What is Reiki doing? As energy flows through the body, harmony is created and imbalances are released. Reiki supports chakra adjustment and balance adjustment. Each chakra is fully functional only if other chakras are also fully involved

HOW DO YOU PURIFY CHAKRAS AND AURAS

Become a goddess: 7 ways to purify the aura

Take a walk in the rain...

Clean the aura by wiping it with a healing herb. ...

Take a cleansing bath. ...

Visualize the other person's aura. ...

Surround yourself with positive energy and keep the aura close to you.

Soak in the sunlight...

Finally, try strengthening the aura with a simple exercise

WHAT SHOULD I EAT TO BALANCE MY CHAKRAS

Food for your chakras

Muladhara

Feed it with: Root vegetables like carrots, potatoes, parsnips, radishes, beets, onions, garlic, and protein rich food like eggs, meats, beans, tofu, soy products, peanut butter

swadhistana

Feed it with: Fan this fiery spot with sweet fruits like melons, mangos, strawberries, passion fruit, oranges, coconut.

WHAT CHAKRA IS FEAR

The third chakra is the Solar Plexus chakra. Located under your ribs and in the diaphragm, this chakra is associated with the color yellow. It is connected to the digestive system and the adrenal acorns. When this chakra is out of balance we experience fears, eating disorders, anxiety, and loss of control.

Made in the USA
Monee, IL
04 January 2020

19876389R00105